Improve your Chess in 7 Days

Gary Lane

BATSFORD

First published in the United Kingdom in 2007 by
Batsford
10 Southcombe Street
London W14 0RA

An imprint of Anova Books Company Ltd

ISBN 9780713490503

A CIP catalogue record for this book is available from the British Library.

15 14 13 12 11 10 09 08 07
10 9 8 7 6 5 4 3 2 1

Reproduction by Spectrum Colour Ltd, Ipswich
Printed and bound by Creative Print & Design, Ebbw Vale, Wales

This book can be ordered direct from the publisher at the website
www.anovabooks.com, or try your local bookshop.

Distributed in the United States and Canada by Sterling Publishing Co.,
387 Park Avenue South, New York, NY 10016, USA

Contents

Dedication

For Ryan and Jasmine

Acknowledgements

With thanks to François Mertens, Jon Manley
and chess historian Edward Winter for their help
in providing material for the book.

Introduction

The chessboard consists of 64 squares on an 8x8 board. You should make sure that the board is set up correctly by checking that the square on the bottom right hand corner (looking at it from the White player's point of view) is light-coloured, which tends to mean white, yellow or beige on most sets.

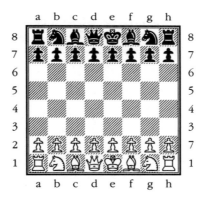

Each piece is represented by a figurine in commentaries on chess games

♙ – Pawn

♘ – Knight or N

♗ – Bishop or B

♖ – Rook or R

♕ – Queen or Q

♔ – King or K

The move of a piece is recorded by the symbol/letter of that piece followed by the square to which it moves. Thus ♗f3 means that the bishop has moved to the f3 square. In case of a pawn move only the square on which it lands needs to be recorded, for example e4 means a pawn has moved from somewhere to the e4 square. A capture is denoted by an 'x'. Thus ♛xb7 means the queen has taken something on the b7 square – and fxe5 means that the f-pawn has captured something on e5.

Characters that have a special meaning in chess

?! A dubious move

? A poor move

?? A blunder that loses material or allows a change in the position such as from winning to losing.

!? Interesting move

! Excellent move

!! Brilliant move

+ Check. At the end of the move. For instance: ♛e2+

0-0 castling kingside

0-0-0 castling queenside

½-½ Draw agreed

1-0 White wins

0-1 Black wins

Day 1

So you want to improve your chess?

Chess Trivia – At Brighton chess club in England during the 1930s, a Mrs Sydney was allowed to bring her dog along – but only if the dog joined the club. Later, the dog, called Mr.Mick, was mistakenly picked for the club's second team. He lost on time....

Chess is fun but it is even more fun when you win!

Though most people will never have enough time to devote to a deep study of chess, it is still possible for anyone to make rapid and significant advances in the game. For example, one way to achieve better results is simply to cut down on your own mistakes while grabbing any opportunity

7

to exploit those of your opponent. Easier said than done, perhaps, but you can train yourself to reach a higher standard by adopting the right attitude.

There is no shortage of chess playing sites on the internet but you should resist the temptation only to play games without thinking and at breakneck speed – *and thereby learn absolutely nothing*. In fact my first words of advice to a friend who wanted to improve was to stop playing for a while. I wanted him to *study chess* a little before playing again and also *record his games* so that he could analyse the moves later with plenty of time to think or consult a computer to check on possible mistakes. He had fallen into the trap of playing games on the internet where speed was often more important than accuracy and purposeful play. Sometimes it did not matter if he was losing on position – so long as he won on time. He had also been playing offhand games occasionally against the same group of players at the local club, where he had not only picked up bad habits but also failed to identify and learn from his mistakes. Nevertheless his curiosity in chess was further aroused when he discovered there were chess openings with weird and wonderful names such as the Frankenstein-Dracula Attack or the Dragon and great chessplayers such as Bobby Fischer and Garry Kasparov. However real improvement came only when he started to *make plans*. This, together with a knowledge of simple opening principles, a grasp of tactical themes and key strategies in the most regularly occurring endgames really did produce results. It may sound too good to be true but with a little guidance players of every level really can make rapid improvement at chess.

How many moves do you think ahead?

This is the question chessplayers are most frequently asked by non-chessplayers – and our suggested answer is seven. Sure, you could try to impress everyone by saying that the number of moves depends on whether the position is a highly complex middlegame or a mathematically precise pawn endgame with few pieces on the board – but why bother? True or false, seven is a good choice. It's a magical number – and chess is truly a magical game. And there is no need to feel guilty about the fact that really you can only see one move ahead, whatever the position. History will provide you with reassurance and comfort. As long ago as 1946 the New York magazine *Chess Review* related what happened when former world champion José Capablanca had just lost a game – which always caused a sensation because it was such a rare occurrence: in fact during one period of his career he didn't lose *for eight years* – 'Apropos is the story of the game between the invincible Capablanca and Charles Jaffe, pride of the East Side. Capa forgot he was invincible: he lost. A reporter who was present asked the Cuban, "How far do you see ahead?" Capa replied impressively, "About ten moves". Then the reporter went over to Jaffe: "How far do *you* see ahead?" Much to everyone's surprise, the reply was, "Only one move". This didn't make sense. "How could a player who can see only one move ahead defeat another who can delve so deeply?" Here Jaffe explained: "I see only one move ahead, *but it is always the best move*".'

Choose the right move

Many attempts have been made to provide players with a procedure for selecting the best move – some of which I find contrived and even impractical. So here I will provide you with very simple but effective steps to encourage you *to think before you move*. However be under no illusions. It is very difficult to control events on the chessboard – which is a wild world where more often than not in the rough and tumble of play "the winner is the player who makes the last but one mistake" as the witty grandmaster Savielly Tartakower once proclaimed.

But you will see an immediate difference in your play if you remember the following:

1 Tactics and predict-a-move

A forcing combination cuts down on calculation – giving you less to think about while you increase the pressure on your opponent. When there are fewer options it is easier to predict the replies, thus enabling you to set a trap with our method and score a quick win if your opponent falls into it.

2 Which alternative?

On the chessboard you will see any number of decent looking moves – so make a shortlist of alternatives by asking yourself the following questions:

Do I need to develop my forces and castle my king into safety?

Is there a threat?

Can I make a threat?

3 Positional needs

Are any of my pieces not taking part in the action — if so how can I move them to better squares?

4 Stick to the plan

Be consistent in your approach. If you think up a plan, stay with it — do not trot out a few moves and then get distracted or abandon it at the first sign of counterplay by your opponent.

5 Stop yourself from making a mistake

Decide on a move but be on the look out for possible danger coming your way, for example:

a) Checks that start a forcing combination against you.

b) Threats to your pieces.

c) Threats of checkmate to your king.

Why bother with tactics?

Tactics are the most spectacular aspect of chess — but not so difficult to learn. They are also the most effective way of deciding a game — either by winning pieces or checkmating the opponent's king.

Trying to work out test positions found in newspaper columns and books can improve your tactical awareness and calculation. It is wrong to assume that solving these puzzles is useless because you are not likely to get those exact positions in your own games. The key to successful attacking play is to

a) Learn the various combinational motifs

b) Learn to identify them when they arise in your own games

This theme will be explored later but a couple of examples spring to mind:

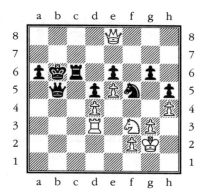

Vallejo Pons – Perelshteyn
World Junior Championship, Yerevan 1999

There is a lot of activity from both sides in this position but White spotted a tactic called in chess parlance a *skewer*. He gave up a rook by **33 ♖b3** upon which Black suddenly resigned because he saw that after the forced 33...♛xb3 – otherwise his queen is lost – there follows 34 ♕b8+ ♚a5 35 ♕xb3 winning the queen and the game.

At first sight this might seem difficult to spot but it will not take long for the motif to stick in your mind and you will be able to notice the possibility of such combinations – and deliver the mortal blow – in your own games. For instance:

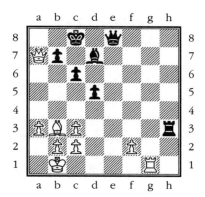

Pintor – Leite
Aveiro 2002

In this position, knowledge of the previous game will help you to find **38 ♖g8!** when 38...♕xg8 39 ♕a8+ ♔c7 40 ♕xg8 leaves White with a winning material advantage.

How to bluff

You would think that it is only the pieces that do the talking in chess. But this is not so. Various forms of psychology are also used at both amateur and master level and are an accepted feature of competitive play. Indeed such ploys can save you from defeat or even completely turn the tables in a desperate situation. A hapless opponent will probably have no idea of what you are up to as he falls headlong into the psychological trap.

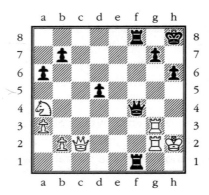

Emms – Ryan
Isle of Man 2003

Here the English grandmaster playing White noticed that his opponent had started to repeat moves by ...♕h4+. So he took the opportunity to get up and stretch his legs with seemingly not a care in the world and the expectation of a shared point by threefold repetition of moves. Well, that's what he *wanted* his opponent to believe – and he did! Ryan peacefully ended the game with **37...♕h4+ 38 ♖h3 ♕f4+ 39 ♖hg3 ♕h4+** and a draw was agreed.

However this was all a cunning ploy by the grandmaster who knew the position was completely lost and his walkabout would put pressure on his opponent to waste no more time but agree a draw. And so he did not have the time to find 37...♖f1-f3! when White actually intended to resign because of the follow up 38...♕h4+ 39 ♔g1 ♖xg3 winning a rook. And 38 ♕g6 protecting the rook also fails to 38...♕h4+ 39 ♔g1 ♖f1 mate.

I asked John Emms immediately after the game how he came up with this clever ruse and he replied: "Some years ago I was playing an American grandmaster when I had a chance to repeat moves. At that very moment my opponent got up and went for a leisurely walk...."

Understanding the openings

It is always useful to vary your opening moves in accordance with the opponent you are playing. It would be foolish to try something completely different – a line in which you have absolutely no experience – but in this era of computer databases a surprise variation can confuse an opponent who has just spent an hour memorising opening moves to play against you but has had no time to *understand* the opening.

In Chapter Two I suggest that to beat a strong player you don't have to raise your game to the level of a world champion and carry out an amazing sacrificial attack, admirable though that may be. Instead I propose a safe opening – but one with the potential to irritate an opponent who will go to any lengths to avoid a draw. In the following game I found myself in just such a situation against a Hungarian grandmaster so played the psychology card – realising that a solid opening would frustrate him because he could not afford to concede a draw if he wanted to challenge for the top prizes:

Lane – Flesch
London 1983

1 e4 c5 2 c3

This pawn push is a solid reply to the Sicilian Defence and has the basic aim of creating a big pawn centre with d2-d4.

2...d5 3 exd5 ♕xd5

Black doesn't mind exposing his queen in the middle of the board because the pawn on c3 prevents White from attacking it by ♘c3 – and gaining time in the process.

4 d4 e6 5 ♘f3 ♘f6 6 ♗e2!?

This departure from the usual 6 ♗d3 appeared to startle my opponent but he continued to rattle out his moves at lightning speed.

6...♗e7 7 0-0 0-0 8 c4 ♕f5?!

On such an exposed square the queen is clearly a potential target but the grandmaster wants to exploit the fact that my bishop is on e2, and not d3, to keep queens on the board. But in doing so Black is already showing signs of recklessness. Objectively, 8...♕d8 is correct and would lead to a middlegame battle or an exchange of queens after 9 dxc5 ♗xc5 10 ♕xd8 (10 ♘c3 gives White a slight edge) 10...♖xd8 11 ♘c3. However a level endgame is not what the grandmaster wants – this is an Open tournament and he needs a win.

9 ♘c3 ♖d8??

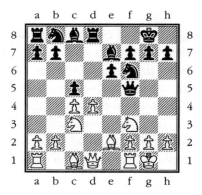

Played without hesitation because the grandmaster assumed the rook on the d-file would force me to defend the d4 pawn. This lack of patience is typical of top players who compete non-stop in tournaments and feel the need to wrap up games against lesser opponents as quickly as possible.

10 ♘h4!

Whoops! Only now does it become apparent that the black queen is lost. The one try is 10...♖xd4 but 11 ♘xf5 ♖xd1 12 ♘xe7+ ♔f8 13 ♖xd1 ♔xe7 leaves him a rook down. A painful lesson for the grandmaster who on move eight should have reconciled himself to a long struggle.

1-0

Strategy versus tactics

Short and sharp tactics are the icing on the cake in chess but sometimes a slower approach is needed – taking your time *to prepare* a situation where you can attack. This is the time when you need to play *positional chess*.

What is it? Well, when there is no obvious way of attacking the opponent and there are no threats coming your way – *Positional chess is the art of improving your own position whilst weakening that of your opponent.*

Once you have achieved sufficient positional superiority always remain on the look out for checks, captures and other threats – they can help you win more games:

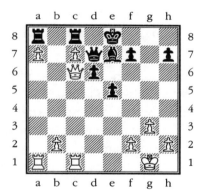

Sulskis – Nick Pert
Port Erin 2003

White has massive positional superiority with two pawns on the seventh rank just itching to promote to a queen. He now switched to pure tactics and found an ingenious way to win:

28 ♕xa8 A queen *sacrifice* but there are two new queens on the way! **28...♖xa8 29 c8=♕+ ♖xc8 30 ♖xc8+ ♕xc8 31 a8=♕ ♕xa8 32 ♖xa8+** with a winning material advantage.

This is all very well, you say – but surely the same theme of vacating a square for a pawn couldn't happen again? No, that is not true. The following position should encourage you to learn the tactical motifs and practice spotting them in practical play.

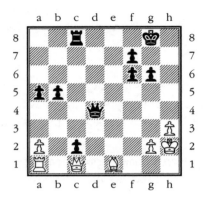

McShane – Richard Pert
British Team Championship (4NCL) 2004

A 'twin' to the previous position – moreover Nick's twin brother had learned the lesson taught by Sulskis to produce an uncannily similar queen sacrifice **34...♕xa1** after which **White resigned** rather than face 35 ♕xa1 c1=♕ when Black has a winning material advantage. So you too can be a brilliant player – just remember combinational patterns.

Creating an attack

A positive mental attitude may be enough to launch an attack right out of the opening but it is more likely that you will first need good positional play to kick start the onslaught.

Lane – Reilly
Australian Open 1999

1 e4 d6

This advance of the d-pawn heralds the Pirc Defence which allows White to construct a big pawn centre, only for Black to attack it later on with blows from his own pawns – and with cooperation from his dark-squared *fianchettoed* bishop which is bearing down on the d4 and e5 squares.

2 d4

And White does indeed take the opportunity to occupy the centre because his pawns control important squares and provide his pieces with room for manoeuvre.

2...♘f6 3 ♘c3 g6 4 ♗e3 ♗g7 5 ♕d2

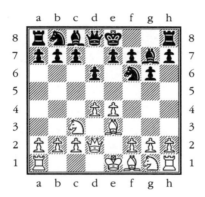

No secret. I am not hiding the fact that I intend to play ♗e3-h6 to exchange Black's important bishop which can be used for both attack and defence. The next part of my plan is to castle queenside and then advance the kingside pawns to open lines in pursuit of the black king.

5...c6 6 ♗h6 ♗xh6 7 ♕xh6

Now the queen is on the h6 square it prevents Black from sliding his king to safety by castling kingside.

7...c5?

Black is keen to distract White from his kingside attacking plans and starts a counterattack on the pawn centre. However moving the pawn twice in the opening loses time and will be severely punished. Instead 7...♕a5 should have been considered.

8 dxc5 dxc5 9 e5 ♘d5

The knight moves out of danger. After 9...♘g4, 10 ♕g7 forces Black to move the rook to f8 after which 11 h3 traps the knight.

10 0-0-0

The knight on d5 is now *pinned* by the rook – if it moves away the black queen will be whisked off the board by the rook.

10...e6

If he protects the knight by 10...♗e6 then White will increase the pressure with 11 ♗c4 and look forward to winning a whole knight.

11 ♗c4 ♞c6 12 ♗xd5 exd5 13 ♞xd5

Even more important than winning the pawn is the fact that I have gained control of the f6 square. The early exchange of dark-squared bishops has left Black defenceless against a knight invasion.

13...♛a5

Getting out of the way, otherwise ♞f6+ would uncover a *discovered attack* on the queen by the rook on d1.

14 ♛g7

Resisting the temptation to play 14 ♞f6+ because there is a mating combination.

14...♖f8 15 ♛f6 1-0

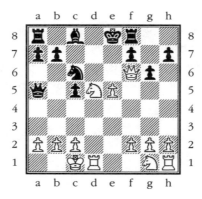

Though my opponent resigned, a spectating fellow-competitor insisted that Black should have carried on and played 15...♗e6. However he was left blushing after being shown 16 ♛e7+! sacrificing the queen for a checkmate after 16...♞xe7 17 ♞f6.

Now you might think that is a very difficult checkmate to spot because the queen sacrifice to mate with a knight looks crazy and would not even be considered by most players. But this is not the case – once you have seen the motif you can remember it and win with it again and again:

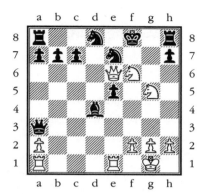

Clemenz – Eisenschmidt
Dorpat 1862

I suspect you will find the spectacular move has now become rather obvious. Yes – the solution is **1 ♕f7+ ♘xf7 2 ♘e6 mate**.

If you are still doubtful that you can train yourself to see such moves then have a go at the following position, taken from a game played over a century later:

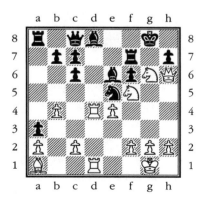

Hall – King
Norrkoping 1988

The move that was hailed as a brilliancy at the time is **1 ♕g7+** but by now it should be clear to you that it is possible to master the art of seeing such moves. **1...♖xg7** is met by **2 ♘h6 mate.**

Avoiding blunders

The clock

Have you ever heard the complaint: "I was two pawns up but lost on time", giving the impression that it wasn't really fair and not that player's fault? The truth however is somewhat different. Nowadays proper handling of the chess clock is an essential part of the game and needs to be taken seriously. There are ways to cope with time-trouble but it is far better to take measures to avoid such a situation altogether. I too have had personal experiences of the dangers of time pressure – which induces blunders that would not normally occur and in an instant can ruin a game that has been carefully nurtured for hours:

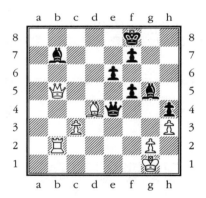

Lane – Van Laatum
Belgian Team Championship 1997

This is from an important game which, had I won, would have put my team at the top of the division. Now I was fairly sure I had made the required 40 moves but to be on the safe side and to put all the anxious spectators' minds at ease I decided to make one more move. My opponent has just allowed me to play 41 ♕xb7 but after a moment's glance it looked somewhat murky after 41...♕e1+ 42 ♔h2 ♗f4+. So I thought – why not stop the bothersome check?

41 ♗f2??

Yes, *anything* can happen in time-trouble.

41...♛xg2 mate

This was played with a loud thud – at which point my team-mates blurted out something in French that sounded like a howl of anguish! So I know from bitter experience the perils of allowing my judgment to be clouded by time-trouble.

Mastering the endgame

Why bother learning more about the endgame when most players know so little about it anyway? Well, as you make progress it is natural to pick up more and more information – and having a few guidelines may help you to score a few more extra points. As they say: a little knowledge is a dangerous thing:

Orr – Vajda
Chess Olympiad, Bled 2002

Playing the white pieces is an Irish player who would have been happy to have made his Romanian grandmaster opponent sweat a little longer but who thought it was now time to bow to the inevitable and agree a draw. I was watching the finish and remember Vajda using psychology to great effect – keeping a straight face and looking remarkably confident.

63 a8=♕+ ♚g1 64 ♕g8+ ½-½

When White offered a draw, Vadja's eyebrows almost jumped up in the air with surprise and his hand shot out for the customary final handshake. As a general rule it is a good idea to make the big guy suffer by playing on in such positions – after all it is difficult to see several moves ahead and you may have missed some hidden winning idea. Moreover if you cannot see how you could possibly lose then why not carry on in such endgames until you have fully satisfied yourself that it really is a draw? Mark Orr is a useful player who must have vaguely remembered that queen versus h-pawn is a draw and – with a large group of spectators gathered around his board – assumed he was wasting the grandmaster's time. But in fact this was not the case. On the contrary we were wondering why the grandmaster was carrying on because crucially the h-pawn is not sufficiently advanced to draw the game.

Play continued **64...♚h1** If 64...♚h2 then 65 ♕g4 wins the pawn because the king must move away from its defence. **65 ♕d5+ ♚g1** 65...♚h2 loses to 66 ♕f3. **66 ♕d4+ ♚h1** Or 66...♚g2 67 ♕g4+ ♚h2 68 ♕f3 and Black must lose the pawn. Now the big difference with having the pawn on h3 is revealed:

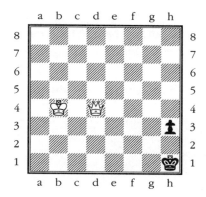

67 ♕f2!

This is what White missed when he agreed to a draw. If the pawn were already on h2 then Black could use it as a device for *stalemate* which would mean the position is drawn as ♕f2 leaves Black without a legal move.

67...h2 68 ♕f1 mate

Now it would be quite a feat to see all this from the position where the draw was agreed – but White had nothing to lose and everything to gain by carrying on.

It should be emphasized that in the endgame it is equally important to look out for checks and threats. There are plenty of opportunities for checkmate or winning material but sometimes players become complacent:

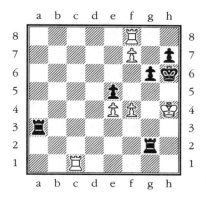

Georgiev – Jakovenko
Wijk aan Zee 2007

The pawn on f7 looks rather ominous but Black has weaved a mating net and now played **50...♖f2!** after which **White resigned** rather than face 51 ♖g1 (51 fxe5 ♖f4 mate) 51...♖xf4+ 52 ♖g4 g5 mate.

The art of swindling

You must make your opponent work hard for victory even though all seems lost. A stunning sacrifice might give you a momentary thrill but if you resign five moves later it has hardly helped the cause. Therefore the key to a good swindle is to frustrate the winning side by putting as many obstacles in his way as possible. In chess the term *swindle* is used to describe how a lost position has been converted into a win or draw. Carrying off a swindle is a sign of resourceful play – as happened here:

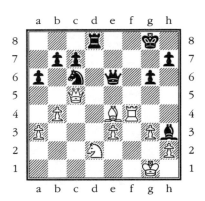

Korchnoi – Krush
Gibraltar 2007

Black has been struggling and after playing 26...g6 the American women's international must have been bracing herself for 27 ♖f8+! when she would have probably resigned in view of 27...♖xf8 (also 27...♔g7 28 ♖xd8 ♘xd8 29 ♕xc7+ is great for White) 28 ♗d5 winning the queen. But instead 'Viktor the Terrible' lived up to his name by making a terrible blunder with **27 ♖f2?? 0-1** The veteran grandmaster realised his error and resigned at once, not waiting for 27...♕xe4! 28 ♘xe4 ♖d1+ 29 ♖f1 ♖xf1 mate. Perhaps the ultimate swindle – the perpetrator did not even have to make a move.

This book is designed to make you think, improve your play – and win more games.

Day 2
Understanding the openings

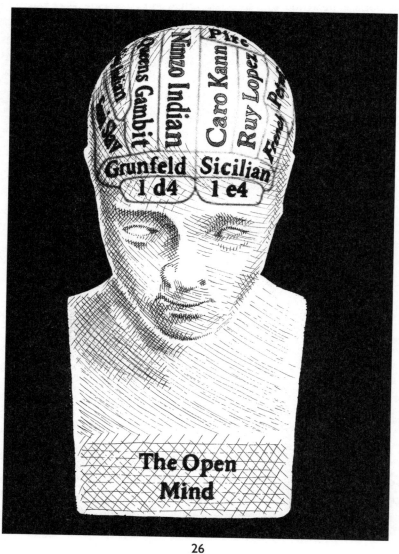

Chess Trivia – The first computer to play in the U.S Open Chess Championship was called Sneaky Pete.

The first few moves of the game are known as the *opening* – although masters have been known to make over 20 moves of theory and still be 'in the opening'. However it is all very well for experts to memorise a baffling number of lines but this is hardly practical for the majority of players. Anyway more important than memory is an *understanding* of your preferred openings.

Then again, everyone has to deal with 'non-book' situations where the opponent will play some previously unplayed or unknown move. In many opening positions there are several good moves but books or DVDs tend to show only one or two alternatives even though there might be other reasonable choices too. Moreover you may be faced with a non-theoretical move that is in fact a howler – and if you can't recall seeing the refutation anywhere then you must find what is wrong with it by yourself. This is where *knowledge of general principles and tactical themes* will serve as your guide so you can emerge from the opening with a decent or even winning position.

1 Develop your pieces

The player who mobilises his army first is more likely to gain the advantage because he will have the initiative and many more attacking options.

2 The first move

In the starting position the only pieces that can move are the knights. To mobilise any of the other pieces you need to advance one or more pawns. The most popular opening moves are 1 e4 and 1 d4 which immediately free the way for the development of both the queen and bishop.

3 Understand the opening

Some players rattle off the first half dozen moves or so from memory and then don't know what to do next. After the fast start you can see them time and again pausing for quite a while trying to work out a possible plan of action. There is a lesson to be learned here. You should first decide on a suitable repertoire and then gain an understanding of your opening choices by referring to a theory book or playing through relevant games with commentaries. Then the basic objectives and tactical tricks associated with the opening will become second nature to you. But always remember that opening theory is published knowledge so a theoretical line could be known to your opponent.

4 Improve your pieces

A good rule of thumb in the opening is *to move each piece only once* in the opening. That way you will mobilise most of your army in the minimum number of moves and without loss of time. Roaming around the board with a lone queen whilst your adversary is developing pieces one after the other is a sure recipe for disaster.

5 Castle

Do not wait too long to castle your king into safety. Whether you castle on the kingside or the queenside your king will then be protected by a wall of pawns. Castling has the added benefit of bringing your rooks into play. An uncastled king in the centre is not only vulnerable to attack but it also prevents the *coordination of the two rooks* – which is an indication that your development has been completed satisfactorily. Though all general principles can be broken under specific circumstances, I always advise inexperienced players to take good care of their king and castle at the first opportunity.

How to choose an opening

When selecting openings for your repertoire you should ask yourself if they suit your own style of play. This may sound obvious but far too often casual players pick up openings by chance rather than considered choice. I once knew a strong player who played quiet lines with 1 d4 as White but defended against 1 e4 with the super-sharp Sicilian Dragon as Black. He invested a huge amount of time learning complicated lines and referred to weekly updates on the internet to keep abreast of new moves played around the world. It was only after years of fruitless endeavour that he finally decided to change his repertoire. Rather bewildered, I asked him why he had tormented himself for so long with an opening that was clearly incompatible with his style? His explanation was that when he was young and looking for an opening, the 'Dragon' sounded exciting. I think we have all kidded ourselves at some point in our lives but you have to be objective and drop any openings in which you do not really feel comfortable. Just because you admire a particularly brilliant win from the Romantic era of chess, that does not mean you have to play the King's Gambit. Nor should you necessarily defend with the Petroff defence just because world champion Vladimir Kramnik employs it as Black. Think about it – with White you are playing a wild attacking game yet with Black you are adopting a dour set up favoured by a grandmaster who wants a draw against a fellow grandmaster.

So an awareness of your style of play and personal preferences will help you decide which openings are best for you. You may not be able to play the opening perfectly but you will get a perfectly playable game. Practically all openings have the same objective: development of pieces and castling the king into safety.

The positional player

Positional players are usually conservative by nature and happy to improve their position little by little and patiently wait for tangible gains. Their overall plan may not be apparent for quite some time but measured and refined preparation will eventually lead to control of the board and a decisive final attack. Masters of this art are former world champion Anatoly Karpov and English grandmaster Michael Adams.

Adams – Spraggett
Hastings 1989/90

1 e4 c6 2 d4 d5

These moves constitute the Caro-Kann defence which is also a great favourite of Karpov. The advance of the d-pawn challenges the centre and clears the way for the development of Black's light-squared bishop.

3 ♘d2 dxe4 4 ♘xe4 ♘f6

Black wants to exchange White's only active piece and have a quiet life. It might seem strange to voluntarily allow the doubling of his pawns but at such an early stage this is not critical. However in a positional sense the pawns may later prove to be a weakness – provided White can find a way to exploit them.

5 ♘xf6+ gxf6 6 c3

White reinforces the d4 pawn rather than play the obvious 6 ♘f3 after which the knight could be pinned by the bishop – 6...♗g4.

6...♗f5 7 ♘f3

Now that the bishop has been developed to the f5 square White decides to bring out the knight as 7...♗g4 would amount to the loss of a move – and the pin would lack menace as the d4 pawn is now well supported.

7...e6 8 g3

A kingside *fianchetto*. The bishop is to be developed on g2 where it will provide extra cover for the white king after castling. Moroever this bishop will find new life on the h1-a8 diagonal.

8...♘d7 9 ♗g2 ♗g7

Black develops his bishop in like fashion but its loss of influence on the queenside will encourage White to launch an offensive there. There is also the downside that on g7 the bishop is obstructed by the doubled f-pawn. However there is a positive side too – on g7 the bishop will provide cover for the black king which might otherwise be exposed to attack on the open g-file after kingside castling.

10 0-0 0-0 11 ♘h4!? ♗g6

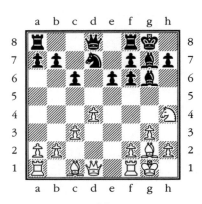

12 a4

The positional player at work. White wants to gain ground on the queenside by a4-a5, thereby also depriving Black of the b6 square for his knight. A further advance of this pawn to a6 will also undermine the c6 pawn and increase the scope of the fianchettoed bishop. Incidentally Adams is not tempted to play 13 ♘xg6, depriving Black of his bishop pair, as after 13...hxg6 Black can soon play ...f5 liberating his dark-squared bishop whilst establishing a solid protective pawn barrier around his king.

On the other hand, playing ...f6-f5 prior to an exchange on g6 would allow White to return his knight to f3 and head for the strong e5 square – highlighting the fact that it is now the bishop on g6 that is blocked in.

12...a5!? 13 ♗f4 ♘b6

If Black activates his queen by 13...♛b6, attacking the b2 pawn, White could reply 14 ♛c1 followed by ♗f4-e3 threatening to hassle the black queen by the discovered attack d4-d5. He also has ♗f4-h6 with a view to exchanging Black's defensive bishop and following up with f2-f4. This would provide White with a dangerous initiative because ...f6-f5, blocking the further advance of the white f-pawn, would leave his own bishop on g6 incarcerated.

14 ♛b3!

Preventing Black's planned knight centralisation by 14...♘d5 which would now allow 15 ♛xb7.

14...♗d3?!

Black jumps at the chance to utilise his bishop to remove White's annoying queen from the b-file. But after the game Spraggett preferred the odd looking 14...♖a6! with the ingenious idea of playing ...♘d5 followed by ♖b6. For example: 15 ♖fd1 ♘d5 16 ♛xb7 would allow Black to win back the pawn by 16...♖b6 thanks to the *double attack* on the queen and b2-pawn. However after 16 ♗d2!, intending the space gaining c2-c4, the bishop-pair provides White with a slight edge.

15 ♖fd1 ♗c4? 16 ♛c2 ♘d5 17 b3! ♘xf4?

Black really should have retreated the bishop with 17...♗a6 – although after 18 ♗c1 it becomes clear that the bishop will remain out of play.

18 bxc4 ♘xg2

After 18...♘g6 19 ♘xg6 hxg6 20 ♖ab1 White's plan would be to treble pieces on the b-file, exerting massive pressure by ♖b3, ♖db1 and ♕b2.

19 ♘xg2

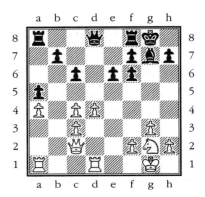

The mini-combination is over and a superficial glance suggests that the position offers no obvious attacking chances. However a strong positional player like Adams knows that it is only White who is able to increase the pressure here. This can be achieved by trebling the heavy pieces on the b-file and returning the knight to the fray by ♘e3 or ♘f4 where it will not only have opportunities for action on Black's light squares but it will also support the pawn advance d4-d5.

19...♕c7 20 ♖ab1 b6 21 d5!?

This pawn thrust is designed to weaken and expose Black's damaged pawn structure in the knowledge that the knight on g2 is ready to leap into action.

21...cxd5 22 cxd5 ♖ac8

22...exd5 would be met by 23 ♘f4, intending ♘xd5, leaving White's knight very powerfully placed and Black's kingside exposed and his bishop doing very little.

23 dxe6 fxe6 24 ♘f4

From this fine outpost the knight can exert pressure on Black's weakened pawns.

24...♖fe8

24...♛xc3 25 ♕xc3 ♜xc3 26 ♘xe6 ♜b8 (otherwise White will play ♜xb6 with a superior endgame thanks to the extra pawn) 27 ♜d7 ♝f8 (27...♝h6 is met by 28 ♘c7 heading advantageously for the d5 square) 28 ♘xf8 ♚xf8 29 ♜xh7 leaves White a pawn up with all the winning chances.

25 ♕b3!

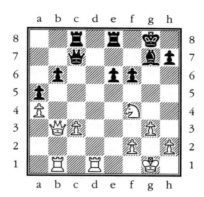

White's position has become stronger move by move. This double attack on the b7 and e6 pawns is the culmination of his masterly strategy.

25...♝h6

In a difficult situation Black pins his hopes on the endgame where he has noticed a line that allows him material parity.

Alternatives are:

a) 25...♛xc3 26 ♕xb6 (or 26 ♕xc3 ♜xc3 27 ♜xb6 e5 28 ♘h5 which also looks good for White) 26...♜c6 27 ♕b7 ♜c7 28 ♕b5 ♜ce7 29 ♘h5 with the superior chances.

b) 25...♛f7 26 ♕xb6 ♜xc3 27 ♕xa5 gives White an extra pawn and much better placed pieces.

26 ♘xe6 ♛xc3 27 ♕xc3 ♜xc3 28 ♜xb6 ♜c4

Black foresaw this position where he is materially level. However he forgot that White also has a number of attacking opportunities – and these soon become evident.

29 ♜d7! ♜c1+

After 29...♜xa4 White can do well with 30 ♘c7! ♜f8 (or 30...♜e1+ 31 ♚g2 ♝g7 32 ♜b8+ ♝f8 33 ♘d5 ♜e6 34 ♜dd8 leading to an easy victory) 31 ♘d5 ♝g7 32 ♘e7+ ♚h8 33 ♘f5 ♖g8 34 ♖bb7 ♖g4 35 ♘h6 winning in style as 35...♝xh6 allows 36 ♖xh7 mate.

30 ♚g2 ♖c2 31 ♚f3

The game is won so Adams can be forgiven this unnecessary king move – presumably made to avoid some vague pressure on his second rank. Immediately decisive would have been 31 ♘c7! ♖ee2 (instead 31...♖f8 32 ♘d5 ♝g7 33 ♖bb7 is crushing) 32 ♖xf6 ♝e3 33 ♖d8+ ♚g7 34 ♘e8+ ♚g8 35 ♘d6+ ♚g7 36 ♖df8 intending ♘f5 mate.

31...♖a2 32 ♘c7 ♖ee2 33 ♖b8+ ♝f8 34 ♚g4 ♖xf2

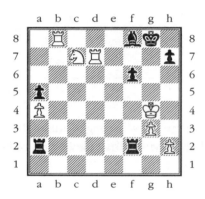

35 h4

White is winning so is no mood to allow a series of checks. However he could have boldly continued 35 ♘e6 when 35...h5+ 36 ♚xh5 ♖xh2+ 37 ♚g6! ♖h6+ 38 ♚f5 ♖f2+ 39 ♘f4 ♖h5+ 40 ♚e6 ♖c5 41 ♖dd8 wins.

35...♖xa4+ 36 ♚h3 ♖aa2 37 ♘e6 1-0

There is no way to avoid mate.

The attacking player

The opening stage is a time to deploy your pieces in anticipation of a middlegame attack. This explains why nowadays sharp tactical lines are favoured, trendy openings embraced and stylish checkmates expected. Masters of the art are Viswanathan Anand, Magnus Carlsen, Garry Kasparov, Hikaru Nakamura, Nigel Short and Veselin Topalov.

Carlsen – Groenn
Norwegian Championship 2005

1 d4 d5 2 ♘f3 ♘f6 3 c4 c6

Black supports the d-pawn and is ready to meet 4 cxd5 with 4...cxd5, recapturing with the pawn in order to keep an equal footing in the centre. If Black ever recaptures by ...♛xd5 then White gains time by ♘c3 chasing away the queen and following up with e4. Alternatively, taking back by ...♘xd5 allows an immediate 5 e4 giving White a big pawn centre. 3...dxc4 is also possible when the opening would be the Queen's Gambit Accepted where White can play 4 e3 or even 4 ♛a4+ to win back the pawn.

4 ♘c3 e6

This position is the starting point of an opening known as the Semi-Slav.

5 ♗g5 h6 6 ♗h4 ♛b6?!

With White's queen's bishop far away from home Black deems it the right time to attack the b2 pawn. 6...dxc4 is usual but Black is trying to confuse his opponent with an offbeat choice. This can be an effective ploy – but only if the move has some use.

7 ♛c2 ♘e4 8 e3

A sensible reply which allows the light-squared bishop to develop and kingside castling to take place. There is no point grabbing a hot pawn by 8 ♘xe4 dxe4 9 ♛xe4?! because 9...♛xb2 allows Black to seize the initiative after 10 ♖d1 ♗b4+.

8...♗b4

The knight is pinned and Black is now ready to castle kingside.

9 ♗d3 ♛a5

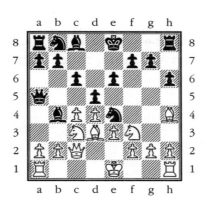

10 0-0!

Teenager Magnus Carlsen is a world class player and gambiting a pawn for a lead in development and an uncastled enemy king is second nature to him. But you might feel the need to weigh up these factors more carefully before embarking on such a sacrifice – however you should also trust your intuition as it plays a major role in chess.

After accepting the pawn, Black's king will remain on its original square and his bishop on c3 will be awkwardly situated. On the other hand White's pieces are well placed, his queen actively deployed and his rooks co-ordinated.

10...♘xc3

Trying to take the pawn *and* exchange queens backfires horribly after 10...♗xc3 11 bxc3 ♕xc3 12 ♗xe4 winning.

11 bxc3 ♗xc3 12 ♖ab1 dxc4

Only twelve moves have been played and Black is already under immense pressure which indicates that the attacking player has chosen the right opening to seize the initiative. Looking at the alternatives helps us to better understand the pawn sacrifice:

a) 12...0-0 13 ♖b3 ♗b4 14 c5 (Not allowing the black bishop to return swiftly to the kingside for defensive duties) 14...♕a4 15 ♕b2 ♗a5 16 ♖b1 intending ♖a3 when Black is in desperate trouble.

b) 12...♗b4 13 c5 b6 14 ♘e5! (a clever idea to launch a lightning attack on the kingside while Black's pieces are marooned on the queenside) 14...bxc5 (or 14...0-0 15 ♗e7 ♖e8?? 16 ♗h7+ ♔h8 17 ♘xf7 mate) 15 ♗g6! 0-0 (15...fxg6 16 ♕xg6+ ♔f8 17 ♕f7 mate) 16 ♗h7+ ♔h8 17 ♗e7 when Black can give up.

13 ♗xc4 ♗b4

Black's problem is that the obvious 13...0-0 allows 14 a3! when the bishop on c3 is embarrassed by the threat of ♖b3, leaving it with no escape square.

14 ♘e5 ♗d6 15 f4

This maintains the momentum by ensuring that 15...♗xe5 can be met by 16 fxe5 opening the f-file for the king's rook to participate in the onslaught.

15...♕c7 16 ♕e4 b6

36

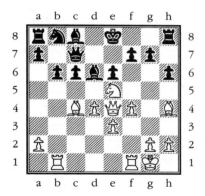

17 ♘xf7!!

A sensational sacrifice to rip apart Black's defensive pawn barrier. Such a daring move was only made possible by Black's failure to *develop and castle*. Not since the eleventh move has Groenn found time to bring another piece into play, whereas White has rapidly improved his position in readiness for a breakthrough.

17...♕xf7

The power of White's well placed pieces becomes apparent on 17...♔xf7 18 f5 ♔e8 19 fxe6 g5 20 ♕g6+ when White has a forced winning combination: 20...♔d8 21 ♖f7 ♗e7 22 ♗g3 ♕b7 23 ♗d6 ♖e8 24 ♖xe7 ♖xe7 25 ♖f1! and Black is mated, e.g. 25...♖e8 26 ♕xe8+ ♔xe8 27 ♖f8 mate.

18 f5

The point of the inspired sacrifice. The f-pawn is advanced to allow the king's rook to enter the fray. Perhaps the key to the success of the attack is the fact that Black cannot safely castle.

18...♕h5

After 18...0-0 19 fxe6 ♕h5 20 e7+ the discovered check is enough to persuade Black to resign.

19 ♗xe6 ♘d7 20 f6

This pawn push throws Black into total disarray. The primary threat is ♗g4+ winning the queen.

20...♘xf6 21 ♖xf6!

Carlsen eliminates the knight which is attacking his queen so that he can once again threaten ♗g4+.

21...♕xh4

Or 21...♗xe6 22 ♕xe6+ ♗e7 23 ♕xc6+ ♔d8 24 ♖d6 mate.

22 ♕xc6+

The time is right for a pretty checkmate.

22...♔e7 23 ♖f7+ ♔xe6

Also 23...♔d8 offers no hope after 24 ♖d7+ ♔e8 25 ♗f7+ ♔f8 26 ♕xd6+ ♕e7 27 ♕xe7 mate.

24 ♕c4 mate

The caveman

The caveman is an all-out attacker. No subtlety whatsoever – the target is the opposing king and the whole opening is geared to deploying his forces in the most hostile manner. This style can lead to stunning victories in 25 moves – but also to shattering defeats. There is a thin line between a properly orchestrated attack and a reckless attempt to checkmate at all costs. I think we have all been there...

Top class cavemen: Alexei Shirov and Mikhail Tal.

Ribli – Tal
Montpellier 1985

1 ♘f3 d5 2 g3

It is worth pointing out that White can lure a careless opponent into unknown territory here. If you normally meet 1 d4 by 1...♘f6 you will be shocked if White suddenly plays 2 d4 leaving you with an 'alien' pawn on d5.

2...♗g4 3 ♗g2 c6

Constructing a pawn barrier on the h1-a8 diagonal in order to reduce the influence of White's light-squared bishop.

4 b3

A safe choice. White fianchettoes *both* bishops. This is all part of a strategy to develop smoothly, castle and then fight for superiority later on in the middlegame.

4...♘d7 5 ♗b2

The bishop prevents Black from expanding in the centre by ...e7-e5.

5...♘gf6 6 0-0 e6 7 d3 ♗c5

A straightforward approach, directing the bishop at the white king.

8 ♘bd2 0-0 9 e4

White has managed to bring his pieces into action and now finds time to advance the e-pawn as a way of gaining space.

9...dxe4 10 dxe4 e5 11 h3

Ribli is happy to gain the bishop pair. Black is now forced to exchange pieces because 11...♗h5 allows 12 g4 ♗g6 13 ♘xe5 winning a pawn.

Later Tal suggested 11 ♕e2 as a possible improvement – with the idea of ♘c4-e3 targeting Black's bishop on g4.

11...♗xf3 12 ♕xf3 ♕e7

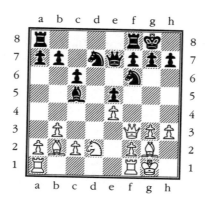

13 ♖ad1

A casual observer might venture the opinion that White is just centralising his rooks. This may be true to some extent but the text is also motivated by Black's last move which contained the positional threat of 13...♗a3, exchanging bishops in a bid to infiltrate later on the weakened dark queenside squares. But now 13...♗a3 can be met by 14 ♗a1 preserving the bishop on the a1-h8 diagonal.

13...b5!

Ruling out the possibility of ♘c4 and intending to generate active play with ...a7-a5-a4 which will also bring the queen's rook into play.

14 h4?!

An ambitious reaction which tries to create some attacking chances on the kingside. The drawback is that without a pawn on h3 Black can eventually plant a piece on g4 with aggressive intent. Instead 14 ♖fe1 offers equal chances.

14...a5 15 c3

An ugly move, obstructing the bishop on b2. However White is preparing to meet 15...a4 with 16 b4, thereby ensuring that the rook on a8 cannot invade his position. Black has played very enterprisingly and now step by step reduces his opponent to abject passivity.

15...♘b6 16 ♖fe1?!

White does not know what to do so makes a waiting move. But the rook move is a poor choice and inspires Tal to exploit the underprotected f2 pawn.

16...♕e6!

A simple but aggressive way to benefit from the weakened g4 square. Black prepares ...♘g4 to target the f2 pawn and will then follow up with ...f5 to unleash the power of the king's rook along the f-file.

17 ♕f5 ♘g4 18 ♖e2

Any hope that an exchange of queens might cut short the attack is doomed to failure: 18 ♕xe6 ♗xf2+ 19 ♔h1 fxe6 with a winning advantage.

18...♖ad8 19 ♗f3

According to Tal's notes, the obvious 19 ♗h3 runs into 19...♖d3 with similar play to the game. However there is an opportunity for a fantastic win which seems to have been overlooked. Black can play 19...♘xf2!! when the game might continue:

a) 20 ♕xe6 ♘xd1+ followed by a capture on e6 winning easily.

b) 20 ♖xf2 g6 21 ♕g4 h5 22 ♕xe6 fxe6 23 ♗xe6+ ♔h7 when the pin on the f-file wins material – especially as 24 ♖df1? allows the decisive 24...♖xd2.

19...♖d3!

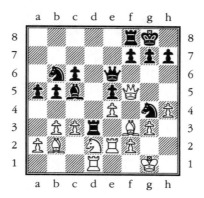

20 ♔g2

The king steps up to renew the attack on the knight. After an immediate 20 ♗xg4 Black wins a pawn and his piece back with the scintillating 20...♖xg3+.

20...♘xf2

A caveman can hardly contemplate playing the sensible but meek ...♘f6 so he goes back to basics and creates a hole in White's defences. The sacrifice may not be 100% correct but it does cause White huge practical problems to solve at the board and the forcing nature of the combination makes it easier for Black to play.

21 ♖xf2

Once again swapping off queens is no use because of 21 ♕xe6 fxe6 22 ♖xf2? ♗xf2 23 ♔xf2 ♖fxf3+ exploiting the pinned knight. Alternatively 21 ♖f1 runs into 21...♕d6 with a clear advantage.

21...♗xf2 22 ♔xf2

22 ♗e2 loses to the spectacular 22...♘d5!, threatening a fork on e3, when 23 ♕xe6 ♘e3+ 24 ♔xf2 fxe6+ 25 ♔g1 ♘xd1 is crushing.

22...♕d6 23 ♗c1 g6

Actually 23...♕c5+, intending ...♕xc3, is the more efficient path to victory.

24 ♕g5 f6 25 ♕h6 f5

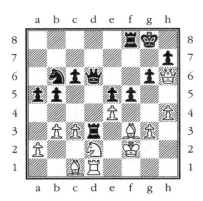

26 ♔g2?

A fatal nudge of the king in the wrong direction which allows an ingenious combination. The unlikely 26 ♔e2 is the best chance, although 26...f4 continues the attack.

26...♖xf3!

Destroying the white king's sole protector. Capitulation is imminent.

27 ♘xf3

The king dies of exposure after 27 ♔xf3 ♛d3+ 28 ♔f2 (if 28 ♛e3 then 28...fxe4+ will win the queen) 28...fxe4+ 29 ♔g2 (or 29 ♔g1 ♛xg3+ 30 ♔h1 ♖f2 leading to mate) 29...♛e2+ 30 ♔h3 ♛xd1 winning comfortably.

27...♛xd1 28 ♘g5 0-1

White decided not to wait for 28...♛h5 or 28...♛d7 which defends against the threat on h7 and leaves Black with a big material advantage.

The pirate

The pirate loves to play openings shunned by the majority of players. These can include oddball lines which stand on the fringe of respectability and others that merely produce smirks of ridicule from opponents. A gambit gives away a pawn but "Why stop there?" says the pirate who is happy to abandon *pieces* in his quest to checkmate. Though the pirate's opening play is characteristically risky he will relish its dubious reputation and count on the element of surprise. And his swashbuckling approach laced with blatant – often unsound – tactics has created many a sensation.

Masters of the art: Everyone will know a pirate in his club, school or local tournament.

Vokac – Bazant
Turnov 1996

1 b4

The Sokolsky or Polish Opening has some pedigree amongst the lesser known openings. White grabs space on the queenside and prepares to fianchetto his queen's bishop.

1...d5 2 ♗b2 ♘d7

The knight is developed as a way of supporting ...e7-e5 and also of reinforcing the knight so that 3 ♗xf6 can be met by 3...♘xf6 without having to double the pawns.

3 ♘f3 ♘gf6 4 e3

This is a reliable method of activating the light-squared bishop. As the black queen's knight is not on c6 it can't be pinned – so the idea is to prepare c2-c4.

4...g6 5 c4 dxc4 6 ♗xc4 ♗g7?

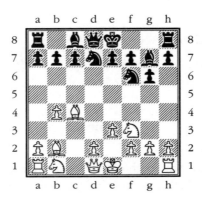

Oops – this is the sort of mistake that gives irregular openings a good name.

7 ♗xf7+! 1-0

Black could not face the bleak prospect of 7...♔xf7 (or 7...♔f8 8 ♘g5 with a clear advantage) 8 ♘g5+ ♔e8 (8...♔g8 allows 9 ♕b3+ mating) 9 ♘e6 when the black queen is trapped.

The ultimate pirate opening is one where material is sacrificed in the opening. A respectable pirate might essay the King's Gambit (1 e4 e5 2 f4) whereas those of the cut-throat variety will happily offer the Blackmar-Diemer Gambit.

Cullum – Wojtowicz
Correspondence 1965

1 d4 d5 2 e4!?

Black is already facing the problem whether or not to accept the gambit. It is amusing to note that this position can even occur after 1 e4 when 1...d5 can be countered by 2 d4. Such obscure openings often have a rich history – in this case Armand Blackmar (1826-1888) from New Orleans popularised the line after writing about it in *Brentano's Chess Monthly* in 1882.

2...dxe4 3 ♘c3

The idea of developing the queen's knight was devised by the keen German amateur Emil Josif Diemer (1908-1990) and quickly caught on amongst gambit players. Blackmar's original idea was 3 f3 but that runs into 3...e5 when 4 fxe4? allows 4...♛h4+ and White is losing.

3...♘f6 4 f3?! exf3 5 ♛xf3?

Racapturing with the queen is very risky and relies on Black going wrong in the complications. 5 ♘xf3 has the merit of preserving the d-pawn and bringing another piece into play – which makes it perfect for games on the internet even if computer analysis has made it hard for White to break down a resolute Black defence.

5...♛xd4

Black accepts the offer and takes another pawn.

6 ♗e3 ♛b4?!

This is such an obvious move that many people have copied it – but trying to enter a winning endgame by 6...♛g4 is a smarter choice.

7 0-0-0 ♗g4?

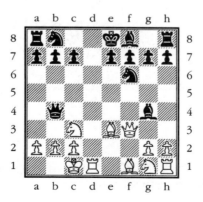

The point of Black's plan. He expects that the attack on the queen will punish White for giving away two pawns and is now patiently waiting for resignation.

8 ♘b5!

There is certainly treasure to be found in the openings if you can play like this. Capture of the queen allows 9 ♘xc7 mate – a tactic that has been known since the 1930s and christened the Halosar trap.

8...e5?

Though it seems sensible for Black to give his king an escape square, the text move proves to be the prelude to a spectacular finish.

Also possible:

a) 8...♘a6 9 ♕xb7 ♕e4 10 ♕xa6 ♕xe3+ 11 ♔b1 and now 11...♗xd1? allows 12 ♕c6+ ♔d8 13 ♕xc7+ ♔e8 14 ♘d6+! exd6 15 ♗b5+ ♘d7 16 ♕xd7 mate.

b) 8...♘bd7 9 ♕xb7 ♕e4 (desperate but 9...♘b6 simply allows 10 ♘xc7 mate) 10 ♘xc7+ ♔d8 11 ♕xa8+ ♕xa8 12 ♘xa8 ♗xd1 13 ♔xd1 when Black should count the pieces and then resign, N.Walker-R.Almond, Jersey 2003.

9 ♘xc7+ ♔e7

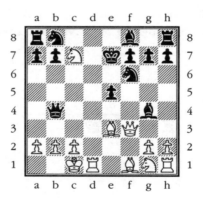

10 ♕xb7!

A chance to win the brilliancy prize is a key motivation for every Blackmar-Diemer Gambit connoisseur.

10...♕xb7

What else?

11 ♗c5 mate

Who are you playing?

ΙΔΕΑ

'Play the man, not the board' is an old adage but one that can help you score points – even against stronger opponents.

In particular you might tailor your choice of opening in accordance with the character of your opponent. For example, if you know that he

47

habitually gets into time-trouble why not adopt an opening that invites complications? He will then go into deep thought, spend too long over the position and run short of time – when he is much more likely to make a mistake. Tailoring your opening play in this way is not difficult – masters and grandmasters do it all the time – so why not you?

For example, Garry Kasparov would spend months working out the weaknesses of his world title challengers and plan his openings accordingly. It is therefore rather ironic that his eventual loss of the title was due to being outfoxed himself in the openings. Vladimir Kramnik made no secret of the fact that he had adopted the Berlin defence because it usually led to an early exchange of queens. And without queens the world's best attacking player ... could not attack! Kasparov was disarmed, failed to win a single game in the match, lost his title and retired from chess a few years later.

A practical life

So try to find out about your opponent's strengths and weaknesses and adapt your opening play accordingly. If you are not sure about your opponent, ask around. It may be easier than you think to gain intelligence. Time-trouble addicts quickly get a reputation as do those who adopt bizarre openings. I once asked a rather distinguished foreign gentleman for a quick opinion on my prospective opponent's play – to which he replied: "Good". After a tedious game I eventually won with an obvious trap. I went up to him afterwards and with a smile on his face he offered me a revised opinion: "Not good!"

If your opponent is a passive, defensive player then confront him with an attacking system. If he is set in his ways and always plays one particular opening – use a move-order trick to get him into unfamiliar territory. And be flexible yourself – break the all-too-common habit of playing the same opening lines irrespective of who your opponent is. Thus if you are faced with a junior who arrives at the board with a laptop case slung over his shoulder, choose a line that you have not employed for a while to nullify any homework he has done on your usual opening preferences.

Beating stronger players

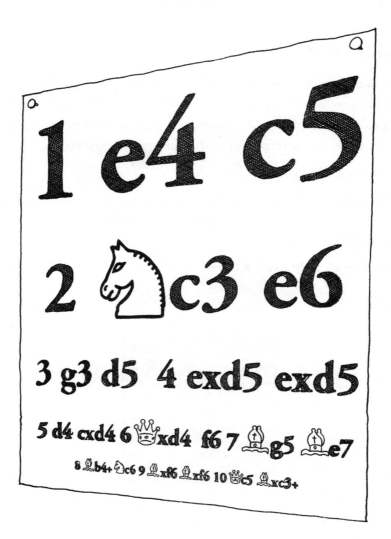

If you want to beat stronger players you must not only have self-belief but also a realistic plan of action. It is all very well to say you are going to bamboozle the highest rated player in the tournament, attack like crazy and then checkmate him with brilliant tactics. If only it were that easy we would all be champions. However one fine day I hit upon another method – to adopt a safety first approach which nevertheless retains latent attacking potential. I found that even grandmasters could get frustrated and lose not only their patience but also their head.

Lane – Nunn
Stroud 1980

1 e4 c5 2 ♘c3

At this time John Nunn was well known for his analytical writings on the complex *open* Sicilian: 2 ♘f3 – so I opted for the solid *closed* Sicilian. As I was a teenager and he a grandmaster, I considered it his job to go for the win and mine merely to get out of the opening in one piece!

2...e6 3 g3 d5

Black strikes at the centre at the earliest opportunity in order to cross White's usual plan of a kingside fianchetto, castling and gradual preparation for an attack.

4 exd5 exd5 5 d4 cxd4 6 ♕xd4

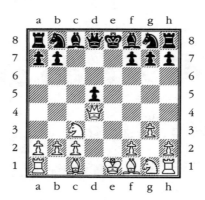

As it happens I was happy to exchange pawns in the centre because already the position is clear enough for me to side-step any tricks and traps in the opening. On the other hand Black now has to find a way to generate activity otherwise I will have the ready-made plan of piling up on the weak isolated d-pawn.

6...♘f6 7 ♗g5 ♗e7 8 ♗b5+ ♘c6 9 ♗xf6 ♗xf6 10 ♕c5

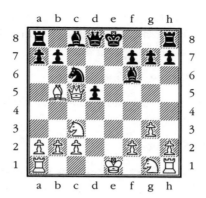

When I played this queen move I could see from Nunn's expression he was not impressed because he knew I was happy to head for an equal endgame. But Black doesn't want an equal endgame nor does he want a draw. Being the tournament favourite, he feels obliged to win in order to make sure of first prize. However this is a hard task in the present position and he will have to take risks to unbalance the game.

Just for the record, Nunn's displeasure was aroused also because he recognised the position as one reached in the Goring Gambit Declined. A pet line of mine which normally occurs after 1 e4 e5 2 ♘f3 ♘c6 3 d4 exd4 4 c3 d5 5 exd5 ♕xd5 6 cxd4 ♗g4 7 ♗e2 ♗b4+ 8 ♘c3 ♗xf3 9 ♗xf3 ♕c4. Here we have the same position as the game but with colours reversed – apart from the fact that White has played the extra move g3 which makes little or no difference.

10...♗xc3+ 11 bxc3

Not 11 ♕xc3 when 11...0-0 when 12 ♗xc6 bxc6 13 ♕xc6? ♖e8+ is fantastic for Black. I am in fact still following accepted practice – at the cost of allowing doubled pawns I have prevented Black from castling. Nunn sees no other way to proceed but to reluctantly allow an exchange of queens.

11...♕e7+ 12 ♕xe7+ ♔xe7 13 0-0-0

The further simplification has seriously reduced any attacking prospects for my opponent. True, I have to keep a constant watch on the doubled c-pawns but Black also has a weakness – the 'isolani' on d5.

13...♗e6 14 ♘e2 ♔d6

The king takes up residence on d6 where it provides protection to the d5 pawn. However Nunn is not satisfied with mere defence and intends to use the king for more active operations.

15 ♖he1 ♔c5 16 c4 dxc4 17 ♗xc6 bxc6

After 17...♔xc6 I can steer the game towards a likely draw by 18 ♘d4+ ♔c7 19 ♘xe6+ fxe6 20 ♖xe6.

18 ♘f4 ♗g4 19 ♖e5+ ♔b4?

In trying too hard to win, Black goes astray. Nunn later revealed that his idea was to place the king on c3 in order to create his own checkmating threats. But all this smacks of frustration, loss of patience and an unjustified refusal to accept the draw.

20 ♖d4!

Now suddenly Black is struggling. The threat is 21 ♘d3+ with a discovered attack on the unprotected bishop – not to mention the fact that Black is on the verge of being mated.

20...♗e6

20...♖ae8 21 ♘d3+ ♔c3 22 ♖xg4 is also hopeless for Black because 22...cxd3 allows 23 ♖c5 mate.

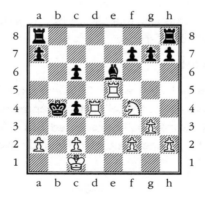

21 a3+!

Though the black king is in a perilous situation anyway, this pawn nudge clinches matters. The combination works because all my pieces are cooperating whereas the lone black king has no support.

21...♔xa3

There is no escape from the mating net: 21...♔c3 22 ♘e2 mate or 21...♔a4 22 ♘xe6 fxe6 23 ♖xc4+ ♔xa3 24 ♖a5 mate.

22 ♘xe6 ♔b4

What else? 22...fxe6 is met by 23 ♖xc4 a5 (to prevent ♖a5+) 24 ♖e3+ ♔a2 25 ♖a4 mate.

23 ♖c5 1-0

So in my first ever game against a grandmaster my 'safety first' strategy worked wonders. And many years later I had the opportunity to pull the same stunt again.

Lane – Bologan
Cappelle la Grande 1992

1 e4 c5 2 ♘c3 e6 3 g3

I am up against a world class player so decided to fall back on the cheeky plan I had adopted against Nunn. This would come as a surprise to my opponent because at this time I was regularly playing 3 ♘f3 and transposing back into the open Sicilian.

The reason for this odd looking move-order is that it provokes confusion. 2...e6 is a popular reply to the Closed Sicilian but if you are an adherent of the Dragon or Najdorf variations which feature 2...d6 you will suddenly find yourself outside your comfort zone. As it happens Bologan plays 2...e6 anyway so I decided on my patent 'safety first' approach.

3...d5 4 exd5 exd5 5 d4 cxd4 6 ♕xd4 ♗e6

Varying from the Nunn game. Defending the d5 pawn with the bishop rather than the knight avoids the pin by ♗g5. It is clear that Black already recognises that he needs to keep all options open.

7 ♗g2 ♘c6 8 ♕a4 ♗b4 9 ♘ge2 a6 10 0-0

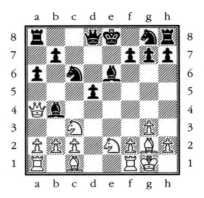

This is new territory for both players but I was happy to have castled and proceeded with my development. In the long-term I will be able to generate play against the isolated d5 pawn but more importantly my grandmaster opponent has no obvious way of disrupting my position at an early stage of the game.

10...♘ge7 11 ♘f4 0-0

It is a matter of taste whether to try 11...♗xc3. In fact doubling the c-pawns is only a short term gain for Black – for example: 12 bxc3 0-0 13 c4 dxc4 14 ♘xe6 fxe6 15 ♕xc4 with the better chances because the e6 pawn is weak.

12 ♘ce2 ♗c5 13 c3

I am not going to allow the d-pawn to advance.

13...b5 14 ♕d1 ♗b6 15 a4 b4 16 cxb4 ♘xb4 17 b3

I still needed to complete my development and saw that a fianchettoed bishop on b2 could target the g7 pawn.

17...♖c8 18 ♗b2 ♗f5 19 ♘d4 ♗e4 20 ♕g4

My first major threat. I am now ready to play ♘e6 with the threat of mate on g7.

20...♘g6 21 ♗xe4 dxe4?

Bologan is all too casual and misses the essential 21...♗xd4 which would maintain equal chances. He must have been confused at my play – in the opening I seemed to be interested only in a safe and sound position but now I am playing like a caveman!

22 ♘f5 ♖c5 23 ♘h5

The double knight attack on the g7 pawn works wonders. On the other hand 23 ♘xg7? allows 23...♖g5! when queen moves allow ...♘xf4 winning and 23 ♗xg7 runs into 23...♖xf5 when 24 ♕xf5 ♔xg7 allows Black to survive the onslaught.

23...f6 24 ♘hxg7 ♕d5

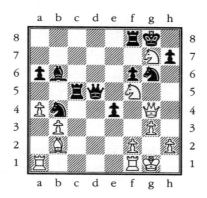

25 ♘e7+! ♘xe7 26 ♘f5+ ♔f7

If Black blocks the check by 26...♘g6 then 27 ♘e7+ wins his queen.

27 ♕g7+ ♔e6 28 ♕xe7+ ♔xf5 29 ♕xf8 ♕c6

Black has a wretched position but plays on in the hope that I will slip up in time-trouble. But I don't.

30 ♗d4 ♘d3 31 ♕g8 h5 32 h3 ♗c7 33 ♕c8+ ♔g6 34 ♕g8+ ♔f5 35 ♗xc5 ♘xc5 36 ♖ac1 ♗d6 37 b4 ♕d7 38 ♕d5+ 1-0

It is a major test to play Nigel Short who was widely regarded as the strongest British player of the 20th century after contesting a world title match against Garry Kasparov in 1993. Nevertheless my strategy remained the same – to play something solid yet with potential and hope that I would so frustrate my opponent that he would go wrong.

Lane – Short
Chess Olympiad, Mallorca 2004

1 e4 e6 2 d4 d5 3 ♘d2 h6!?

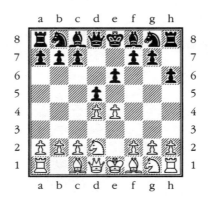

I was slightly shocked but at the same time amused by this move. Eager to avoid a draw, Short has a nagging feeling that he might run into opening preparation if he follows the main lines. Hence the reason for playing something unusual. In fact 3...h6 has also been adopted on occasion by a few other adventurous world class players.

At this point I vaguely recollected one of Short's games from Gibraltar 2003 where he defended a similar position against Pavlovic. The game went 3...c5 4 ♘gf3 ♘f6 5 exd5 ♘xd5 6 ♘b3 ♘d7 when White played 7 ♗g5 – so I guess you could argue that at least this move has been ruled out by the unusual move order.

4 c3

A flexible response which helps to support the d4 pawn.

4...c5 5 ♘gf3 ♘f6 6 exd5 ♘xd5 7 ♘b3

7 dxc5 might also be considered in order to open some lines. After 7...♘d7 8 ♗c4 ♘xc5 9 0-0 gives White a slight edge because he has more room to manoeuvre his pieces to better positions.

7...♘d7 8 ♗d3 ♕c7

A simple developing move which equalizes because of the threat of ...c4 forking the knight and bishop.

9 &c2 b6 10 0-0

I had not played this line before but kept faith in the basic policy of *develop and castle* to avoid any pitfalls in the opening.

10...&b7 11 &e1 &e7 12 &e5 &xe5 13 dxe5 0-0-0

It makes sense to sharpen the position by queenside castling. The immediate threat is 14...&xc3 with a discovered attack on the queen, so I have to take evasive action.

On the other hand Black must not play 13 ...0-0? because White has a direct attack with 14 &g4 threatening &xh6. Then 14...&h8 15 &h5 &g8 (or 15...&ad8 16 &xh6 gxh6 17 &xh6+ &g8 18 &h7 mate) 16 &xh6! (ripping open Black's defence – a logical sacrifice when you consider that White's queen's rook and bishop are also ready for action) 16...gxh6 17 &xh6 f5 18 c4 &b4 19 &e3 (intending &g6+ and &h3) is very strong.

14 &g4 h5 15 &c4 g5

Black rightly tries to create the right conditions to attack on the kingside and distract my attention from any queenside activity. However there is no obvious threat since Black has not yet deployed sufficient forces on the kingside.

16 a4 a6

Black realises my intention is to play a4-a5 and is ready to meet it by ...b5, driving back the white queen.

17 &d2 &b8 18 &ad1

An all-out attack on the queenside will not quite work so I decide to develop my rook in the centre where it has more influence.

18...g4 19 &c1 &dg8 20 &e4

Now that Black is ready for action I place my bishop on the h1-a8 diagonal to neutralise any potential danger from the bishop on b7. The policy of frustrating the grandmaster's attacking attempts works well here.

20...h4

The e-pawn is taboo because after 20...&xe5 21 &xd5 &xd5 22 &f4! (the key move which pushes Black to the brink) 22...&xc4 23 &xe5+ &c8 24 &xh8 with a clear advantage.

21 &d3 g3 22 h3

Attention to defence. By blocking the advance of the h-pawn I minimise any disruption to my kingside pawn structure. My idea is to contain any activity directed against my castled position and then turn my attention to the queenside. Of course, 22 hxg3? is a mistake because after 22...hxg3 Black has excellent chances of checkmate along the h-file after a future doubling of rooks.

22...gxf2+ 23 ♘xf2 ♛xe5?

A big shock as I had assumed this move was not possible. However, as shown by the previous two games, the stronger player can become frustrated with a passive position and act rashly in a radical attempt to change the situation. I had the impression that Short was supremely confident about his position because he had left the board and didn't come back for ages. Moreover this is the position that attracted the attention of most spectators – who assumed I was in deep trouble because the earlier defensive plan of 24 ♗xd5 ♗xd5 25 ♗f4 no longer works due to 25...♖xg2+ 26 ♔h1 (26 ♔f1 allows 26...♗xc4 with *check* announced in a loud voice) 26...♖xf2+ 27 ♖xd5 ♛xf4 and White can resign.

24 ♗xd5 ♗xd5

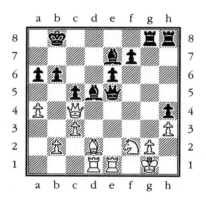

25 ♛xd5!!

Though this may look crazy it is actually a spectacular winning move – which leads to a decisive advantage in the endgame. After the game I found out from one of the English players that Short's disappearance from the board was due to the fact that after playing his last move he had immediately spotted his error and didn't want his body language to reveal anything. By that I presume he meant the look of horror on his face!

25...♛xd5

If 25...exd5 then 26 ♖xe5 leaves White a piece up.

26 ♗f4+ ♗d6

After 26...♚c8 then 27 ♖xd5 exd5 28 ♖xe7 is similar to the game – the active white rook gives Black serious headaches.

27 ♗xd6+ ♚c8 28 ♖xd5 exd5 29 ♖e7

White has a very favourable endgame because the passive position of the black king makes it easy for me to conjure up tactics – especially if I can add the knight to the attack.

29...♖h6 30 ♗f4 ♖hg6 31 g4

To prevent Black's rooks chasing away my king from the g2 square.

31...hxg3 32 ♘g4

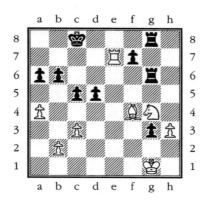

I have managed to fend off Black's initial flurry of activity and now Short has a dour defensive task in prospect.

32...♖8g7 33 ♚g2 d4 34 cxd4 cxd4 35 ♗e5 d3

This is a good example of the resourcefulness shown by top players. If White takes the rook then the d-pawn promotes.

36 ♖c7+!

The easiest way to keep guard over the troublesome d-pawn is to bring the rook into the action. In time-trouble I noticed that 36 ♗xg7 allows the trick 36...♖xg4 when after 37 hxg4 d2 I can't stop the pawn from queening. Later I did find a draw by 38 ♖e8+ ♚c7 (38...♚d7 39 ♖e4 d1=♕ 40 ♖d4+ wins) 39 ♖e7+ ♔c8 (or 39...♔c6 40 ♗e5 d1=♕ 41 ♖c7+ ♔d5 42 ♖d7+ ♔xe5 43 ♖xd1 and Black can resign) 40 ♖e8+ ♔c7 41 ♖e7+ with a repetition.

36...♔d8 37 ♖c3 ♖xg4

This is desperate but other lines are also bleak: 37...♖g8 38 ♗f6+ ♔e8 (if 38...♔d7 then 39 ♘e5+ is a killer fork) 39 ♖xd3 when suddenly the threat of mate in one wins the remainder of his pieces.

38 ♖xd3+ ♔e7 39 hxg4 ♖xg4 40 ♖d4

I am a piece up but even the best players in the world take their time resigning in the hope of a mistake by their opponent – especially if he happens to be in time-trouble.

40...♖g5 41 ♗f4 ♖g6 42 ♗xg3 a5 43 b3 ♖c6 44 ♖c4 ♔d7

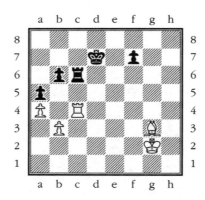

45 ♔f3

I did not have to spend any time spotting the winning idea – which is to increase the role of the king. But there is a need to be careful. The obvious 45 ♖xc6?? would be a tragic error of judgement – even if it does seem natural to exchange when you are a piece up. Short had craftily spotted that 45...♔xc6 46 ♔f3 b5 draws because of 47 ♔e4 (or 47 axb5+ ♔xb5 48 ♗d6 a4 49 b4 a3 50 ♗e5 ♔xb4 51 ♔f4 with a clear draw) 47...bxa4 48 bxa4 and the bishop is of the wrong colour diagonal to force the promotion of the a-pawn.

45...♖f6+ 46 ♗f4 ♖c6 47 ♔e4

The game continues – but all I have to do to secure victory is to make sure I don't lose on time.

47...♖e6+ 48 ♔d5 ♖f6 49 ♗e5 ♖f3 50 ♖c7+ ♔d8 51 ♖c3 ♖xc3 52 ♗xc3 ♔d7 53 ♗e5 f5 54 ♗f4 1-0

Day 3
Strategy versus tactics

Chess Trivia – In New York 1857 Paul Morphy, the best player of his day, played Louis Paulsen. They decided to record the times for any move over 5 minutes. Morphy, renowned for his brilliance, consumed 25 minutes but his opponent used up a whopping 11 hours.

Though you may have a preference for tactical play you can't expect to deliver one brilliancy after another and assume combinational positions from your games will end up in a *Find the Winning Moves* puzzle book.

So you must also pay attention to *strategy* – which is characterised by *planning* so you can achieve some goal or other, whether it be in the short or long term. It is a most important aspect of the game – after all you have to play well positionally to get your whole army in place before you unleash those wonderful attacks.

So when there is no sign of tactics you should gradually improve your position or weaken that of your opponent. Keep yourself busy in quiet periods of the game and look for a piece that is doing very little – it may even still be sitting on its original square – and try to bring it into the action. It is important not to make useless moves, whether it be pushing a random pawn or shuffling your king from side to side, because that is a sign you are drifting and not playing purposefully.

Predict-a-move

Predict-a-move – so often overlooked by improving players – is a proven method of winning more games. Quite simply you try to anticipate what your opponent is about to do next and then find a move that conceals a deadly trap if he just blindly carries on with his plan.

You can often catch someone out by finding a move that looks like it is merely improving your position – but which in reality introduces a tactical trap. For instance:

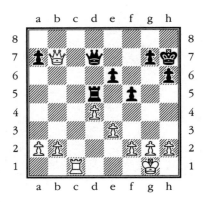

Position from a game played between two amateurs
Yugoslavia 1949

In reaching this position, Black knew that his opponent would never be able to resist playing **1 ♖c7?** 'winning the queen' – because if she moves then ♖xg7+ mates in two – but when he did so he was rocked by the prepared trap **1...♖c5!!** which completely turns the tables. Black threatens a *back rank mate*: 2 dxc5 ♕d1 mate or 2 ♖xd7 ♖c1 mate, while 2 ♖xc5 is met by 2...♕xb7 when Black's material advantage wins easily.

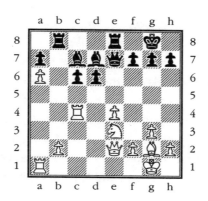

Schuermans – Lane
Le Touquet 1991

White has just taken a pawn on c4 with his rook and has a readily available tactical plan of 23 ♘d5, meeting 23...cxd5 with 24 Rxc7. Bearing this in mind I found a move that set a trap whilst at the same time improving my position. I played **22...♖b5** and my opponent suspected nothing because the idea seemed solely to be the doubling of rooks on the b-file by means of a future ...♖eb8. There followed: **23 ♘d5?** whereupon **23...♖xd5!** exploited the pin on the e-file and left White a piece down.

Even the opening can go wrong as was the case in **Nohut – Vandevoort**, Belgian Team Championship 2002: **1 e4 c5 2 c3 d6 3 d4 ♘f6 4 dxc5** 4 ♗d3 is the solid alternative. **4...♘c6** Not 4...♘xe4?? – amazingly this is a frequently made mistake – since 5 ♕a4+ wins the knight on e4. **5 ♗c4!?** A sharp idea designed to provoke complications **5...♘xe4 6 ♗xf7+ ♔xf7 7 ♕d5+ e6 8 ♕xe4 d5 9 ♕f3+ ♕f6 10 ♗e3 ♘e5 11 ♕e2 ♕f5**

63

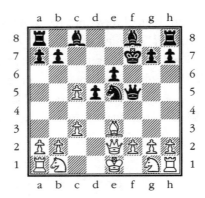

The obvious intention of playing the queen to f5 is to continue ...♘d3+. However White sees this coming and quietly brings another piece into the game with **12 ♘f3** whereupon Black automatically continues with his plan of **12...♘d3+?** thereby allowing **13 ♕xd3!** Only now does it become clear that *predict-a-move* worked a treat because **13...♕xd3** is met by **14 ♘e5+** winning back the queen and leaving White a piece up. **1-0** !

After the previous basic examples we now look at slightly more sophisticated methods which are even more likely to lure the unwary to their doom:

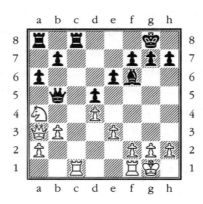

In the game **Qendro – Shaw**, Chess Olympiad, Turin 2006, White has just advanced the b-pawn against his higher rated opponent. The straightforward idea is to play ♖xc8 followed by ♖c1 and a draw offer. The Scottish international now showed his guile by letting White get on with his idea – because he had spotted something rather special. **17...♕a5!** Shaw lays his trap. All will soon be revealed. The queen shift is a useful move anyway – because it prepares ...b7-b5 exploiting the pinned knight.

18 ♖xc8+ ♖xc8 19 ♖c1 ♖c2!

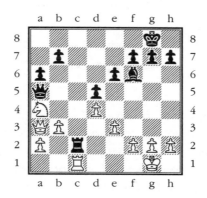

A stunning reply that was concocted a few moves ago with the *predict-a-move* method. Black seems to offer his rook for nothing but then 20 ♖xc2 reveals the point of ...♕a5 – 20...♕e1 mate! The other tactical point is the threat of ...♗e7 deflecting the white queen from its defence of the rook. **20 g3** White avoids the back rank mate. If 20 ♖f1 then 20...b5 wins because the knight is pinned. **20...♗e7 21 ♕xe7 ♖xc1+** And the material advantage led to victory for Black. The game continued: **22 ♔g2 ♖c8 23 ♕xb7 ♖e8 24 ♘c5 ♕b5 25 ♕xa6 ♕xa6 26 ♘xa6 ♖a8 27 ♘b4 ♔f8 28 ♔f1 ♔e7 29 ♔e2 ♔d6 30 ♔d2 g5 31 a4 ♖g8 32 ♘d3 f6 33 b4 ♖g6 34 b5 ♖h6 35 a5 ♖xh2 36 b6 ♔c6 37 ♘b4+ ♔b7 38 ♘d3 ♔c6 39 ♘c5 ♖xf2+ 40 ♔c3 ♖f1 41 b7 ♔c7 42 a6 ♖a1 43 ♔b4 h5 44 ♔b5 ♖b1+ 45 ♔a5 h4 46 ♘xe6+ ♔b8 47 ♘d8 hxg3 48 ♘c6+ ♔c7 0-1**

I used *predict-a-move* to my advantage in the following game which once again demonstrates how effective this method can be:

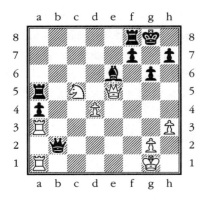

Solomon – Lane
Oceania Zonal, Auckland 2005

In this position White has just played 29 ♖ga3 with the obvious intention of capturing the a4 pawn. A *predict-a-move* scenario – so I set a trap. **29...♖d8** This works well because it looks like my only concern is the d4 pawn but that hardly conflicts with White's obvious reply. **30 ♖xa4?** Why not? Because of... **30...♖xc5!** This is what I was planning – to divert the white queen away from the kingside so I could attack. **31 ♕xc5** Of course 31 dxc5 is ruled out by 31...♕xe5. **31...♗d5!**

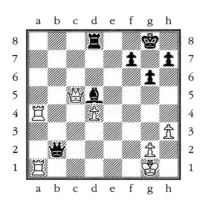

It suddenly dawned on White that there is no satisfactory way of defending against the threat of checkmate on g2. I had to play 29...♖d8 to make sure that the bishop was protected on d5. White managed to struggle on for a few moves but is a hopeless task. **32 ♖1a2 ♗xa2 33 ♕a5 ♕c1+ 34 ♔h2 ♕f4+ 35 ♔h1 ♖c8 0-1**

It is time to see how the *predict-a-move* method worked in a recent game.

Howell – Nasri

World Junior Championship, Yerevan 2006

1 d4 d5 2 c4 e6 3 ♘c3 c6

This is the Noteboom variation of the Semi-Slav defence. The idea is that if White continues with 4 cxd5 then Black plays 4...exd5. The difference from Queen's Gambit lines is that there is no black knight on f6 so ♗g5 is not an immediate option.

4 e4 dxe4 5 ♘xe4 ♗b4+ 6 ♗d2

This Marshall Gambit surrenders the d-pawn in return for a strong initiative where the black queen is chased around the board. It was first played by Marshall against Schlechter, Monte Carlo 1902 and the experts are still debating who is better.

6...♕xd4 7 ♗xb4 ♕xe4+ 8 ♗e2

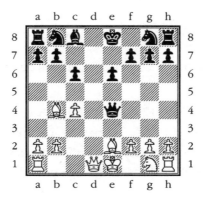

White offers another pawn – happy in the knowledge that his lead in development will ensure tactical chances.

8...c5!?

Though this is well known, nowadays 8...♘a6 is the fashionable move. After 9 ♗d6 the game Borovikov-Porper, Senden 2006 continued: 9...e5 10 ♘f3 ♗g4 11 0-0 0-0-0 12 b4 ♘f6 (12...♘xb4!? is worth a try) 13 c5

♘d5 14 ♖e1 ♘c3? (exchanging pieces by means of this fork seems sensible but Black has missed something) 15 ♗xa6! ♗xf3 (if 15...♘xd1 then 16 ♖xe4 wins material) 16 ♕b3 ♕g4 17 ♗f1 gave White a winning position in Borovikov-Porper, Senden 2006.

9 ♗xc5 ♕xg2 10 ♗f3

The bishop defends the rook and shoos away the queen.

10...♕g5 11 ♗a3

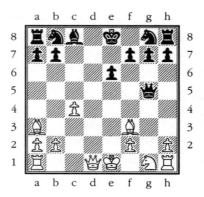

The bishop retreats and in some cases White is ready to follow up with ♕d6.

11...♘d7

Rather belatedly Black fears that his pieces will be reduced to the role of mere spectators.

Also possible is 11...♘e7? 12 ♘e2 ♘f5?! (perhaps 12...♘bc6!? should be tested) 13 ♖g1 ♕d8? (13...♕f6 is met by 14 ♕d2 intending to castle queenside with bright prospects) 14 ♕xd8+! ♔xd8 15 0-0-0+ ♔c7 (or 15...♘d7 16 ♘d4 ♘xd4 17 ♖xd4 e5 18 ♖d6 intending to double rooks on the d-file with an excellent game) 16 ♘d4! ♘xd4 17 ♖xd4 ♗d7?! (Black is trying to catch up on development but this is simply wrong) 18 ♖xg7 ♗e8 19 ♗d6+ ♔c8 20 ♖h4 h6 21 ♗h5 ♘d7 22 ♗a3 ♘b6 23 ♗xf7 ♗xf7 24 ♖xf7 1-0 Jobava-Portisch, Rethymnon 2003.

12 ♘e2 ♘e5!? 13 ♘c3

13 ♗e4, intending ♖g1, looks like a decent alternative.

13...♘e7 14 ♘e4 ♘xf3+ 15 ♕xf3

This position is fine for White with his unopposed bishop exerting nagging pressure along the a3-f8 diagonal – something which makes it virtually impossible for Black to castle kingside. In this difficult position Black must defend accurately.

15...♕a5+ 16 ♔f1 ♘f5 17 ♖d1 ♕a4

Though the obvious move is 17...♗d7?, to prepare ...0-0-0, it backfires in dramatic fashion: 18 ♖xd7! ♔xd7 19 ♘c5+ (the start of a king hunt) 19...♔e8 20 ♕xb7 ♖d8 21 ♕c6+ ♔f8 22 ♘b3+ when Black can give up.

18 ♕d3 ♕d7 19 ♕e2 ♕c6

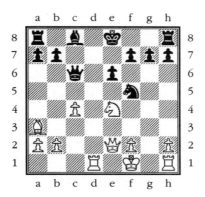

20 ♖d6!

A classic continuation using the *predict-a-move* method. Black has already shown his readiness to accept any material on offer by grabbing a couple of pawns so he will hardly be able to resist this rook – especially as there is no obvious checkmate in sight. The conventional way to maintain the advantage is 20 ♖g1 – but that wouldn't scare Black.

20...♘xd6?

This totally justifies Howell's imaginative play. 20...♕c7 would have been more sensible.

21 ♘xd6+ ♔d7

Black's pieces lack co-ordination and his king is badly exposed.

22 ♖g1

Before continuing with the onslaught White moves his rook out of danger. Black underestimated this 'quiet move' and now can only sit and watch as White's attacking options rapidly increase.

22...♖g8

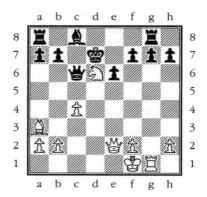

23 ♘xf7

The teenage grandmaster is spoilt for choice. 23 ♕d3! also promises a spectacular finish in view of the threat of discovered check: 23...♚c7 (or 23...♚e7 24 ♘e4+ ♚e8 25 ♘f6+! gxf6 26 ♖xg8 mate) 24 ♘b5+ ♚b6 25 c5+! ♚a5 26 b4+ ♚a4 27 ♘d4 and mate will soon be forced.

23...♕b6

23...♚e8 does not help. White responds 24 ♘h6 when 24...♖f8 25 ♖xg7 wins.

24 ♕d3+ ♚e8 25 ♘d6+ ♚d7 26 ♘f5+ 1-0

Initiative

When you are attacking or putting your opponent under pressure you *have the initiative*. This can be crucial because when you are in the driving seat you are more likely to be able to carry out a forced tactical sequence:

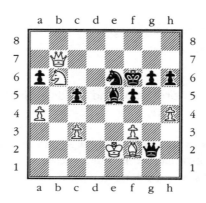

Miles – Lane

British Championship 2001

A knife edge position has been reached where at first sight it is difficult to see who exactly has the initiative as both sides are on the attack. In fact I am threatened with checkmate in one move by 39 ♘d5 – but thankfully it is *my* move and this gives me the chance to exploit my initiative and commence a forcing combination. The key factors on my side are the exposed white king and the fact that my queen is well placed to attack. There followed: **38...♘f4+** The knight covers the d5 square but more importantly the white king is now forced to take a walk around the board. **39 ♔e3** Instead 39 ♔e1 ♗xc3+ leads directly to mate after 40 ♔d1 ♕f1+ 41 ♔c2 ♕d3+ 42 ♔b3 ♗d4+ 43 ♔a2 ♕c2+ 44 ♔a3 ♕b2 mate. **39...♗d4+!** The only way to force the white king into the open board. Even though I only have a queen and knight in hot pursuit it is enough because White's pieces are too far away to provide any form of cover. **40 cxd4 cxd4+ 41 ♔xd4** If 41 ♔xf4 then White is mated with a pawn after 41...g5+ 42 hxg5+ hxg5 mate. **41...♕xf2+ 42 ♔c4 ♕c2+ 43 ♔b4** The king cannot escape by 43 ♔d4 due to 43...♘e6+ 44 ♔d5 (or 44 ♔e3 f4 mate) 44...♕c5 mate. **43...♘d3+**

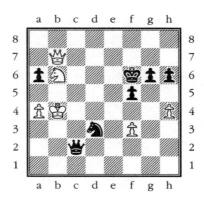

44 ♔a5 If 44 ♔a3 then 44...♕b2 mate. **44...♕d2+ 0-1** After 45 ♔xa6 comes the knight fork 45...♘c5+ winning the queen.

An easier version of the awesome power of a forcing combination is the following endgame where White uses his initiative to deliver checkmate:

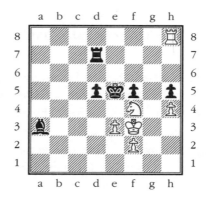

Kuzubov – Van Beek
Gibraltar 2007

White finished smartly with the forcing **57 ♖h6!** threatening 58 ♖e6 mate. This was enough for Black to resign because on 57...♖d6, stopping the rook mate, comes a mate with the knight instead – 58 ♘d3 mate.

Strategy

72

You can use strategy where a positional plan is necessary to improve your position. Subtle manoeuvring, placing pieces on mysterious squares and patiently provoking pawn weaknesses can seem a daunting task but do not be dismayed – you are probably already playing strategically when you move up your queen to a menacing attacking position and follow up with a flank pawn advance to create a point of entry in the opponent's castled position...

But it is probably easier to see how a small positional advantage can lead to a substantial plus:

Karpov – Kasparov
Game 17, World Championship Lyon/New York 1990

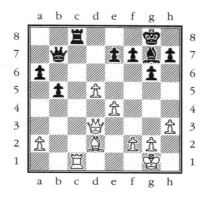

This is a typical example where the paths of positional play and tactics come together to improve a position. Here Black has just played ...Ic8 to which the obvious answer is to exchange rooks and quickly agree a draw. However White finds a way to maintain the tension:

26 Ic6! ♗e5

The problem with exchanging rooks is that 26...Ixc6 27 dxc6 gives White a strong passed pawn – thereby condemning Black to miserable defence after 27...♕c7 (or 27...♕xc6 fails to 28 ♕d8+ ♗f8 29 ♗h6 winning easily) 28 ♕d7 ♗e5 29 ♗b4 e6 30 ♕e8+ (this is just fantastic for White who can gleefully chase the black king) 30...♔g7 31 ♕f8+ ♔f6 32 ♕h8+! ♔g5 33 ♗d2+ ♗f4 34 h4+ ♔xh4 35 ♕f6+ ♔g4 36 f3+ ♔h5 37 g4+ and it is finally time for Black to admit defeat.

27 ♗c3 ♗b8

In the space of a few moves it has become obvious that Black has been reduced to passivity and now has little freedom of choice. After 27...♗xc3 28 ♕xc3 (White controls the c-file and if the black rook moves off the line then ♖c7 is very strong) 28...♖xc6 29 ♕xc6 White's queen dominates the board and there is an impending threat of e4-e5 which will help create a passed d-pawn.

28 ♕d4 f6 29 ♗a5

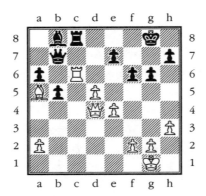

29...♗d6

Even the great Garry Kasparov can't conjure up a magical solution and must sit tight in his wretched position and adopt a wait-and-see policy. As previously, the pawn cannot be won because after 29...♖xc6 30 dxc6 ♕xc6 31 ♕d8+ ♔f7 32 ♕xb8 White has a clear advantage. Instead 29...♕d7 encourages 30 ♕c5 – an echo of the actual game where White dominated the c-file and tried to force an exchange of rooks: 30...♖xc6 31 ♕xc6 ♕d6 32 ♕e8+ (the start of a king hunt) 32... ♔g7 33 ♗d8 ♕h2+ 34 ♔f1 ♕h1+ 35 ♔e2 ♗h2 36 ♕xe7+ ♔h6 37 ♕f8+ leads to a forced mate after 37...♔h5 38 g4+ ♔g5 39 ♕xf6+ ♔h6 40 ♕f8 mate.

30 ♕c3 ♖e8

Black finally concedes control of the c-file and is helpless to prevent White from steadily improving his position.

31 a3 ♔g7 32 g3

Maybe 32 &c7! is the best choice. Black would then have to worry about 32...&xc7 33 &xc7 &b6 34 &c6 &b7 35 e5 when White has a clear advantage.

32...&e5 33 &c5 h5 34 &c7

Karpov decides the time is right to exchange Black's only active piece.

34...&a1

So Black has avoided the exchange of pieces – but at a hefty cost because now the bishop is out of play.

35 &f4 &d7 36 &c7 &d8

The end of a bad day for Kasparov as 36...&xh3 allows 37 &xe7+ &xe7 38 &xe7+ &g8 39 &h6 which leads to mate.

37 d6 g5 38 d7 &f8 39 &d2 &e5 40 &b7 1-0

I am quite sure many people would carry on but Kasparov is wise enough to realise he can do little against the simple plan of &c6 followed by &e3-b6 winning hands down.

Years later the same positional trick to avoid exchanges was acclaimed as truly insightful. However a little knowledge can work wonders...

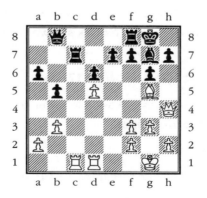

Kramnik – Aronian
Chess Olympiad, Turin 2006

20 ♖c6!

No prizes for guessing the key move – but it is a gentle reminder of how history can repeat itself. A canny player can watch out for such positional nuances to help convert a probable draw into a win. 20 ♗xe7 is tempting but then 20...♖e8 21 ♗f6 (21 ♗xd6? is calamitous because of 21...♖xc1 22 ♖xc1 ♕xd6 winning a piece) 21...♕c8 gives Black active play.

20...♖xc6?

It seems that this response might have some merit because the c-pawn may be rounded up later and captured. However in reality this is not so easy and in the meantime White can use the passed pawn to force Black on to the defensive. Aronian should have instead considered 20...♖fc8 when 21 ♖dc1 e6 offers equal chances – however over-the-board pressure can induce even the world No. 3 to go wrong.

21 dxc6 ♖c8 22 ♖c1 e6 23 ♗d2 ♕c7

The queen is awkwardly placed here but otherwise White plays 24 ♗a5 and advances the c-pawn one square further. If 23...♕b6 then 24 ♕e7 is hard to meet. After 24...♕c7 (not 24...♖xc6? allows 25 ♕e8+ winning) 25 ♕xc7 ♖xc7 26 ♗a5 ♖c8 27 c7 intending ♖c6 gives White a winning endgame.

24 a4

Now that Black is preoccupied with halting the advance of the c-pawn, it makes sense for White to weaken Black's pawn structure so he can then infiltrate his camp.

24...d5 25 axb5 axb5 26 ♕b4 ♖b8 27 ♕a3

White switches his queen to the a-file in order to threaten ♗a5 – once again Black has practical difficulties.

27...♗d4 28 ♕a6 ♗e5

After 28...♖b6 29 ♕a5 White threatens ♗e3 to exchange bishops which would then enable the tactic ♕xb6! when ...♕xb6 allows c6-c7 winning.

29 f4 ♗d6 30 ♗a5

White has succeeded in his strategy of forcing the queen to give way and this heralds the further advance of the c-pawn to the seventh rank.

30...♛c8 31 ♕a7 ♖a8 32 ♕b6 ♖b8 33 ♕d4!

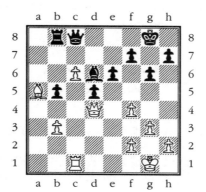

The centralised queen is striking out in every direction and though it has been chased away from the queenside where it was trying to assist the advance of the c-pawn, it is now perfectly placed for action on the a1-h8 diagonal.

33...b4

Preventing ♗c3 when the queen and bishop battery threatens mate on g7 or h8.

34 c7 ♖a8

After 34...♖b7 follows 35 ♕f6 when the killer ♕d8+ is hard to meet, especially as 35...♗xc7 loses to 36 ♕e7.

35 ♕b6 ♗f8 36 ♗xb4 ♗xb4 37 ♕xb4 ♕e8 1-0

How many moves in a plan?

A plan refers to a *series* of moves to improve the position, not one solitary move. Naturally, when you start planning you can go through the rules outlined in Chapter One, paying particular attention to forced moves and threats from your opponent. After you have satisfied yourself that there is no spectacular tactic to hand and that there is no *predict-a-move* available then comes the time to think. This is the moment when most mistakes occur because the temptation is to wait and see what the opponent is up to by moving any piece just for the sake of it. This is the wrong attitude – but you can significantly improve your performance by simply taking a little time deciding which piece is contributing the least and then trying to improve its position.

Benko – Botvinnik
Monte Carlo 1968

1 c4 g6 2 g3 ♗g7 3 ♗g2 e5 4 ♘c3 ♘e7 5 e4 d6 6 ♘ge2

There is a touch of irony here in that Benko is employing the Botvinnik system of the English Opening – against Botvinnik himself!

6...♘bc6 7 d3

It is worth noting that White is playing the Closed Variation of the Sicilian Defence with colours reversed and an extra move. The argument being that the move in hand makes little difference. Just for the record the usual move-order is as follows: 1 e4 c5 2 ♘c3 ♘c6 3 g3 g6 4 ♗g2 ♗g7 5 d3 d6 6 ♘ge2 e5.

7...f5 8 ♘d5

The knight moves to a square of influence and if Black employs copycat tactics and places a knight on d4 then it can easily be shooed away with c2-c3. Also possible: 8 0-0 0-0 9 ♘d5 (9 ♗e3!? is met by 9...♘d4 to stop the possibility of a timely d3-d4) 9...fxe4 (I think this reduces Black's options such as ...f5-f4 so it is not as popular as Botvinnik's handling of the opening – meanwhile 9...♗e6 10 ♗e3 ♕d7 leads to the main game) 10 dxe4 ♗e6 11 ♗e3 ♕d7 12 ♕d2 ♖f7 13 ♖ad1 ♖af8 14 f3 led to equal play in Stokke-Hammar, Stockholm 2006.

8...0-0 9 ♗e3 ♗e6

At the moment the position hardly looks dangerous for White but Black is engaging in positional chess by improving his pieces before contemplating an attack. The bishop comes to e6 in order to allow the queen to occupy the d7 square so that the rooks can be co-ordinated. This will form the prelude to a middlegame plan based on the doubling of rooks on the f-file.

10 ♕d2 ♕d7 11 0-0 ♖f7 12 ♖ac1 ♖af8 13 f4

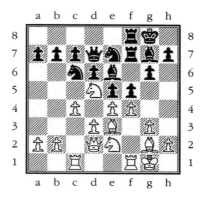

The position seems to be tense but what should Black do with no obvious breakthrough in sight? In his notes to the game Botvinnik made it all seem so easy by outlining a plan and then carrying it out. First of all the idea is to exchange pawns on e4 when White is obliged to take back with the d-pawn otherwise a knight occupies the useful f5 square. The next stage is to exchange the light-squared bishops with ....♗h3 in order to weaken control of the e4 pawn and expose the white king. Then the intention is to exchange pawns on f4 when White will take back with the g-pawn in order to have some control over the e5 square. This will allow Black to continue with the task of undermining the e4 pawn with a rook on e8 and when a knight defends it from g3 then comes the advance ...h7-h5, highlighting the weakness of the e4 pawn and exploiting the open position of the white king.

13...fxe4 14 dxe4 ♘c8!?

This might look strange but if you know the plan to undermine the e4 pawn it is logical. The idea is to play ....♗h3 but if White takes on h3 the queen would have to recapture, leaving the c7 pawn to its fate. Therefore the knight retreat is designed to cover the c-pawn because the rook on f7 is now defending it.

15 c5 ♗h3 16 b4 ♗xg2 17 ♔xg2 exf4 18 gxf4 ♖e8 19 ♘g3

This is all part of Botvinnik's plan and is the obvious continuation because it provides extra cover for the white king, while at the same time defending the e4 pawn. 19 ♘ec3 is less impressive after 19...♘d8, intending ...c7-c6 trapping the knight and giving Black the better of it.

19...h5

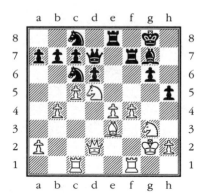

The plan has been smoothly executed by Botvinnik and the various positional themes have enabled Black to create a situation where there is scope to start an attack.

20 b5

Though it looks awkward, necessary is 20 h4, preventing the advance of the black h-pawn – although the game remains complicated after 20...♛g4.

20...♞6e7 21 f5 h4 22 fxg6 ♜xf1 23 ♜xf1

If 23 ♞xf1 then 23...♛g4+ 24 ♚f2 ♞xg6 gives Black winning chances because the e4 pawn is weak and the white king badly exposed.

23...hxg3 24 ♜f7

Instead 24 ♝h6 is met strongly by 24...♛g4! attacking the e4 pawn. After 25 ♜f4 ♛xg6 26 ♝xg7 gxh2+ 27 ♚xh2 ♞xd5 28 ♛xd5+ ♚xg7 wins comfortably.

24...♝e5!

Botvinnik maintains his advantage by holding on to his key defensive piece. Instead a casual move such as 24...♛e6? courts disaster by 25 ♜xg7+! ♚xg7 26 ♝d4+ ♚g8 (26...♚xg6 allows the knight fork 27 ♞f4+ winning the black queen) 27 ♞f6+ ♚f8 28 ♛h6 mate.

25 ♗d4 ♕g4

The rook is offered as a sacrifice in the knowledge that 26...♗xf4? allows 27 ♘f6+ winning instantly.

26 ♖f4

Or 26 ♗xe5 gxh2+ 27 ♗g3 ♕xe4+ 28 ♔xh2 ♕xg6 29 ♘xe7+ ♘xe7 favouring Black.

26...♕h5

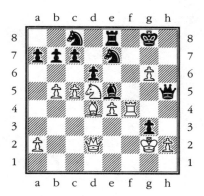

The big threats are 27...♕xh2+ and 27...♘xd5 to prepare ...♗xf4 when the game is over.

27 ♗xe5 ♕xh2+ 28 ♔f3 ♕xd2

Black has a material advantage but White struggles on – more in hope than anything else.

29 ♘f6+ ♔g7 30 ♘xe8+ ♔xg6 31 ♖f6+ ♔h7 32 ♗xg3 ♕d3+ 33 ♔f2 ♕xb5

It is time for White to count the pieces because the knight cannot move due to the threat of ...♕b2+, while 34 ♖f8 looks useless after 34...♕c5+.

34 cxd6 ♕xe8 0-1

Naturally strategy and tactics tend to go hand in hand. In the following game White gets a grip on the position, makes it awkward for Black to develop and then delivers a neat tactical finish to win in style.

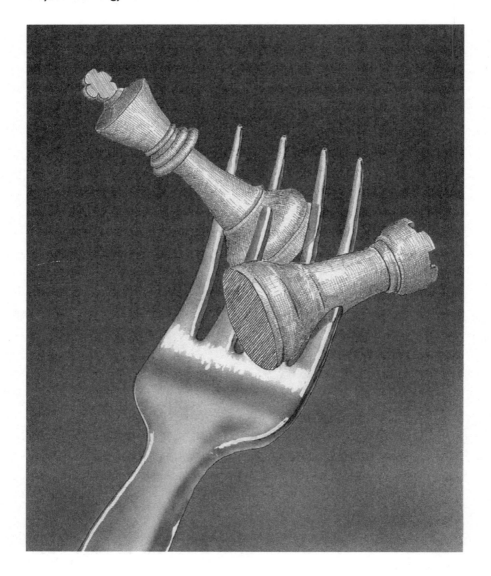

Xie – Larsen
Monaco 1994

1 e4 g6 2 d4 ♗g7 3 ♘c3 c6

This pawn advance provides Black with flexibility. He can follow up with
...d7-d5 making it a Caro-Kann or play ...d7-d6 which is a Pirc.

4 ♘f3 d6 5 h3

Xie Jun, women's world champion at the time, already takes steps to restrict Black's movements by preventing ...♗g4 pinning the knight.

5...♘f6 6 a4 0-0 7 ♗e3 ♘bd7 8 ♗e2

Again we see the tried and tested policy of *develop and castle*.

8...e5 9 dxe5!? dxe5 10 0-0 ♕e7 11 ♕d3 a5

Black makes an effort to stop White gaining more space on the queenside.

12 ♕c4 ♖e8 13 ♖fd1

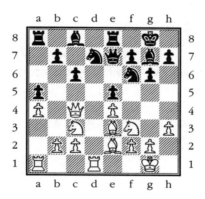

13...h6?!

The start of a clever but flawed plan to transfer the knight vis f8-h7 to g5 or even e6. However this manoeuvre is very time consuming and in the meanwhile White can proceed to improve her position. After 13...♕b4 comes 14 ♘g5! when 14...♖f8 15 b3 h6 16 ♘f3 ♕xc4 17 ♗xc4 gives White a great endgame as it is easier for her to manoeuvre the pieces to better positions.

14 ♘d2

This may look odd but the idea is to move the queen, play ♘c4 and infiltrate with the white knight on d6.

14...♘h7 15 ♕b3 ♘g5 16 ♘c4

White has managed to get a knight to the useful c4 square, whereas the opponent's knight on g5 has not helped to improve Black's position one bit.

16...♘c5?

Larsen targets the queen and e4 pawn but has missed a tactical point as the queens can now be forcibly exchanged. An improvement is 16...♘e6, although 17 ♘d6 maintains White's advantage.

17 ♕a3 ♘ce6

Instead 17...♘cxe4? runs into trouble because of the line 18 ♕xe7 ♖xe7 19 ♘xe4 ♘xe4 20 ♘b6 ♖b8 21 ♖d8+ ♚h7 22 ♖xc8 winning.

18 ♕xe7 ♖xe7 19 ♘b6

The knight exerts a powerful influence by restricting Black's queenside pieces – in particular the light-squared bishop will have difficulty in moving.

19...♖b8 20 ♗g4! ♖e8

The rook retreats in preparation for ...h7-h5 which if played immediately would allow 21 ♗xg5 hitting the rook and winning.

21 ♗xg5!

White exchanges pieces in order to keep a grip on the game. Black has a hard time getting his pieces into action.

21...hxg5

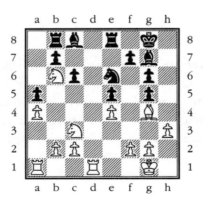

22 ♘b1!

A wonderful strategy to bring the knight into the action via d2-c4 where it will increase the stranglehold on Black's position.

22...♗f8 23 ♘d2 ♗c5 24 ♘dc4 ♗xb6 25 ♘xb6

Black has exchanged one of the knights but is still saddled with a terrible position where he can hardly move a piece without losing material.

25...♔f8 26 ♖d2 ♔e7 27 ♖ad1

Step by step Xie Jun has patiently improved her position. But now that her strategy has succeeded in restricting the movement of Black's pieces, she has to look for a tactical finish.

27...♖f8 28 ♘xc8+ ♖fxc8 29 ♖d7+ ♔f6

29...♔f8 is marginally better even if 30 ♗xe6 fxe6 31 ♖h7 ♔g8 32 ♖dd7 leaves White well on top.

30 ♗xe6 fxe6 31 g4!

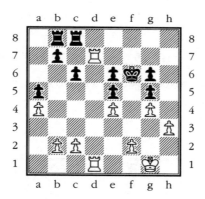

1-0

Black resigned rather than face the stylish ♖1d3 and ♖f3 mate.

The strategy of improving the position of a knight to assist in a final tactical solution is also the theme of the following game:

Ftacnik – Lane
Australian Championship, Brisbane 2006

1 d4 f5

This opening is known as the Dutch Defence. It tends to go in and out of fashion because not many of the top players favour it. However, it has been employed by former world champions Alekhine and Botvinnik so it has gained some degree of respectability.

2 ♘f3 ♘f6 3 g3 g6 4 ♗g2 ♗g7 5 b3 0-0 6 ♗b2

I knew in advance that my grandmaster opponent from Slovakia preferred this solid set-up which is supposed to stifle Black's intended piece development. However this did not deter me because I knew that White had a lot to do if he wanted to win quickly – and I was in the mood for a long fight.

6...d6 7 0-0 ♕e8

The queen helps prepare a future ...e7-e5 and in some cases can move to the g6 or h5 squares to promote an attack after the g-pawn advances.

8 ♘bd2 ♘c6 9 ♘c4 e6 10 a4 h6 11 e3 g5 12 ♘e1 a5

I wanted to restrain White's queenside pawn advance although the text does make it easier for White to exploit the b5 square now that ...a6 has been ruled out.

13 ♘d3 b6 14 ♘a3 ♗b7 15 ♘b5 ♖c8 16 c4 ♘d8

The knight goes into reverse gear in a bid to exchange White's important defensive g2-bishop.

17 f3

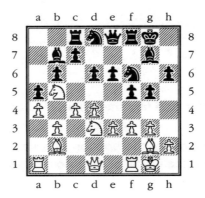

17...♘f7!

I now carried on with my plan to activate the queen's knight but I later found out that Ftacnik had missed the idea of ...♘h8-g6. Despite the time spent on this manoeuvre it just about works because the position is so locked that White has no immediate possibility of a breakthrough.

18 ♗a3 c5 19 ♖a2 ♕e7 20 g4 ♘h8 21 ♖e1 fxg4 22 fxg4 ♘e4 23 d5?

Ftacnik spots a tactic and tries to lure me into a trap by offering a pawn. 23 ♘f2 is the sensible choice and provides equal chances.

23...exd5 24 cxd5 ♘g6

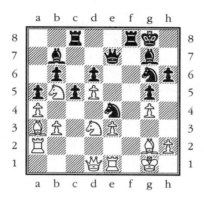

In keeping with the strategical plan, the knight is brought back into the action and increases Black's influence on the kingside by preparing ...♘h4. Instead 24...♗xd5? justifies White's tactics due to 25 ♘f2! ♗c6 26 ♗xe4 ♗xe4 27 ♘xe4 ♕xe4 28 ♘xd6 winning because of the fork of the queen and rook.

25 ♘f4

Noticing that I was getting into time-trouble, White complicates matters by offering me a knight for next to nothing.

25...gxf4 26 exf4 ♘xf4 27 ♖xe4

Or 27 ♗xe4 ♘h3+ 28 ♔g2 ♕h4 with a strong attack.

27...♗e5 28 ♗b2 ♕f6 29 ♗xe5 dxe5 30 ♘c3

White is in trouble due to his weak d-pawn and the powerful black knight on f4 but he carries on defending as best as he can in order to place obstacles in my way.

30...♖cd8 31 ♖d2 ♖f7 32 ♖e3 ♘xg2 33 ♖xg2 ♖df8 34 h3 ♕f4 35 ♕d3 ♔h8 36 ♖e4?

Ftacnik knows the position favours Black so he rushes his moves in my time-trouble. However it backfires because now I have the opportunity to gain a big advantage.

36...♕c1+ 37 ♔h2 ♖f3 38 ♘e2

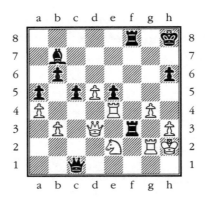

I did not see this move coming but decided to simplify as I thought it was the safest route to victory.

38...♖xd3?!

A little more time might have helped me to find 38...♕f1! Carrying on attacking is the best plan of action since 39 ♖e3 (if 39 ♕c2 then 39...♖f2 leads to mate) fails to 39...♗xd5! threatening ...♖xe3 and ...♕xg2 mate and winning easily.

39 ♘xc1 ♖d1 40 ♖g1

White gets into more trouble but if the knight moves then ...♗xd5 will win the exchange.

40...♖f2+ 41 ♔g3 ♖xg1+ 42 ♔xf2 ♖xc1 43 ♖xe5 ♗a6??

This throws away the advantage and makes the endgame a candidate for inclusion in the final chapter on swindles. The first thing I saw was 43...♔g8! 44 d6 ♖d1 45 ♖e8+ ♔f7 46 ♖e7+ ♔f6 47 ♖xb7 ♖xd6 drawing but I missed the fairly obvious 44...♗c6! which prevents the advance of the d-pawn and brings the game to an abrupt halt in view of 45 ♔e2 (otherwise ...♖d1 will round up the passed pawn) when 45...♖c2+ 46 ♔d3 ♖f2 intending ...♖f6 wins comfortably.

44 ♖e6 c4

The game now fizzles out to a draw.

45 bxc4 ♗xc4 46 ♖xh6+ ♔g7 47 ♖xb6 ♗xd5 48 ♖b5 ♗c6 49 ♖xa5 ♖c2+ 50 ♔g3 ♖c3+ 51 ♔h4 ♗g2 ½-½

Day 4
Creating an attack

Chess Trivia – US president Gerald Ford officially declared October 9th as National Chess Day.

There are some chess players who always seem to be able to create an attack even in positions which look quite harmless. So it helps to know the pre-requisites and principles governing the preparation and execution of a successful attack. By playing through the games and examples in this book you will notice that certain attacking themes and motifs occur again and again – and by absorbing these and introducing them into your own games you will significantly improve your level of play.

General rules

1 Exploit the opponent's weaknesses.

2 Eliminate the opponent's strengths.

3 Detect typical mating patterns and combinational motifs.

4 Remove your own weaknesses.

5 Promote your strengths.

Opposite sides castling

You might assume that when the two opponents castle on opposite sides and go for each other's king, the first to launch an attack will win. However this is not necessarily the case since not only is expertise and accuracy required to invade an enemy position and checkmate the king but also a fair amount of luck. Moreover the opponent might launch a counter-offensive which will have to be put down before completing one's own final assault.

There are few players who have won over chess fans like former world champion Mikhail Tal. His entertaining play and dazzling attacks cast a magic spell and brightened up the chessboard. Contemporaries saw him as a one-off chess genius – but, even so, it is possible to emulate some of his brilliant methods.

Tal – Koblencs
Riga 1957

1 e4 c5 2 ♘f3 d6 3 d4 cxd4 4 ♘xd4

The present position is standard for the 'open' Sicilian and offers Black a variety of ways to develop, depending on his taste and style.

4...♘f6 5 ♘c3 ♘c6 6 ♗g5

This is known as the Richter-Rauzer variation after two players – one German and one Russian – who advocated the line in the 1930s.

6...e6 7 ♕d2 ♗e7 8 0-0-0 0-0 9 ♘b3 ♕b6 10 f3

The f-pawn not only supports e4 but also prepares g2-g4 with a possible pawn storm on the kingside. This scheme of play is well known to masters and is all about whose attack arrives first. If the defender plays too passively and his counterattack lacks punch he could find himself in big trouble.

10...a6 11 g4 ♖d8 12 ♗e3 ♕c7 13 h4 b5?! 14 g5 ♘d7

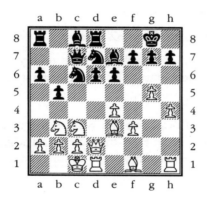

15 g6!

A striking pawn sacrifice that forces the opening of lines against Black's castled position. If the pawn is refused then pawn takes pawn check will follow – if it is accepted then White pushes his h-pawn to h5 and a file will be opened for the king's rook. A routine player might plod on with an immediate h4-h5-h6 – but this achieves nothing as Black can then block the kingside by ...g6 making an attack more difficult.

15...hxg6

You would think that the present day Sicilian clan would have learned from Tal's games and avoided this position at all costs – but this is not so. The line is still being tested – as in the game Short-Muir, Catalan Bay 2004 where play continued 15...fxg6 16 h5 gxh5 17 ♖xh5 ♘f6 18 ♖h1 (perhaps 18 ♖g5 is also worth investigating) 18...b4 19 ♘a4 ♖b8 20 ♕f2 ♖f8 21 ♕g1 with worrying attacking chances.

16 h5 gxh5 17 ☖xh5 ♘f6 18 ☖h1!?

The rook returns to its original square to allow the queen to get in front of it and do serious damage on the h-file.

18...d5?!

Opening the h2-b8 diagonal so as to meet White's threatened ♕h2 with a queen exchange – but Tal has a ready retort. Maybe 18...♘e5 is more accurate to bring another piece over to defend the kingside.

19 e5?!

Tal's caveman temperament, coupled with a wonderful imagination, leads him to sacrifice another pawn to enable ♕h2. Nevertheless it seems that a better way to do this was by 19 ♗f4! when 19...♗d6 20 ♗xd6 ♕xd6 21 f4 threatens e4-e5 after which ♕h2 is again on the cards – without fear of a queen exchange.

19...♘xe5 20 ♗f4 ♗d6 21 ♕h2 ♔f8

The startling 21...♘d3+ looks impressive until you see 22 ♔b1! when Black must stop the checkmate in one after which the knight *can* be taken.

22 ♕h8+ ♘g8?

If you have plenty of time you can work out that 22...♔e7 is the best chance but in the heat of an over-the-board attack and with limited time on the clock it is extremely difficult for the defender to cope with all the threats.

23 ☖h7 f5 24 ♗h6

A marvellous position – so typical of Tal's attractive style. The bishop is immune to capture because of the double pin – against king and queen. Black's defensive resources are being stretched to the limit.

24...♖d7

Breaking the pin – now the bishop *is* threatened.

25 ♗xb5!

Tal may be making magic but he also does logic too. There are now two bishops under attack by pawns but neither can be safely taken. The second bishop offer clears the way for White's queen's rook to transfer to the g-file where it will place the g7 pawn in mortal danger.

25...♖f7

Black just moves the rook out of the bishop's line of fire.

Also possible:

a) 25...♖e7 26 ♖g1 ♖a7 27 ♗e2 is good for White.

b) 25...axb5 26 ♘xb5 ♕b7 27 ♘xd6 ♖xd6 28 ♗xg7+ and it's time for Black to quit.

c) 25...♘g6 looks like it wins the queen in the corner – but 26 ♘d4 threatening 27 ♘xe6+ keeps the attack raging.

26 ♖g1 ♖a7 27 ♘d4!

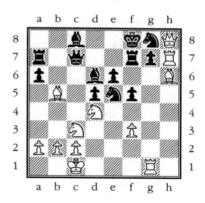

27...♘g4

Just to give you some idea of the checkmating possibilities in this position, here is a sample line: 27...♘c4 28 ♘xf5! ♗f4+ (or 28...exf5 29 ♘xd5 ♕b7 30 ♗xc4 is winning) 29 ♔b1 exf5 30 ♘xd5 ♕e5 31 ♗xc4 ♗xh6 32 ♖xh6 ♕d4 33 ♖gh1! (intending ♕xg8+ and then ♖h8 mate) 33...♖fd7 34 ♕xg8+ ♔xg8 35 ♘e7+ ♔f8 36 ♘g6+ ♔e8 37 ♖h8 mate.

28 fxg4 ♗e5

Alternatives can be handled with confidence by White:

a) 28...♗f4+ 29 ♗xf4 ♕xf4+ 30 ♔b1 ♕xd4 31 ♖gh1! and once again the threat is ♕xg8+ followed by mate.

b) 28...gxh6 29 gxf5 ♗f4+ 30 ♔d1 ♗g5 (or 30...♗g3 31 ♖xf7+ ♕xf7 32 ♖xg3 wins) 31 ♖xh6 ♕f4 32 ♖xg5 ♕xg5 33 ♖g6 and Black can resign.

29 ♘c6 ♗xc3 30 ♗e3!

The bishop is now poised to deliver a knockout blow by checking on the c5 square. If 30 ♘xa7 then 30...♕xa7 hits the rook on g1 and can be followed by ...axb5, making victory more difficult for White.

30...d4 31 ♖gh1!

Relentless attacking. The latest trap is 32 ♕xg8+ ♔xg8 33 ♖h8 mate. That may have been enough to snare the average player but Koblencs is a quality opponent.

31...♖d7 32 ♗g5! axb5

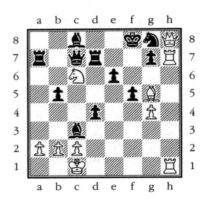

33 ♖1h6!!

Do not adjust your chess set because this really happened. I would have been ecstatic if I had been playing White in this game – and immediately made enquiries about the $10,000 'Best Game Prize'. But not Tal – he used to play like this all the time! The intention is to play 34 ♖f6+ gxf6 35 ♗h6+ when Black's position collapses.

33...d3 34 bxc3 d2+ 35 ♔d1 ♕xc6 36 ♖f6+ ♖f7

After 36...gxf6 White has a crushing attack: 37 ♗h6+ ♖g7 38 ♗xg7+ ♔e7 39 ♗xf6+ ♔d6 40 ♗e5+ ♔d5 41 ♗b8 and the threat of ♕e5 decides.

24...罝d7

37 ♕xg7+ 1-0

Though few, if any, can play like Tal, it is possible to look at such games and learn the tricks of the trade. In the next game French chess magazines raved over White's 14th move, but after seeing Tal's brilliancy it should come as no surprise to us:

Apicella – Collas
French Team Championship 1996

1 e4 c5 2 ♘f3 e6 3 d4 cxd4 4 ♘xd4 ♘f6 5 ♘c3 d6 6 ♗e3 ♗e7 7 f3 ♘c6 8 ♕d2 0-0 9 ♗c4 a6 10 0-0-0 ♘a5 11 ♗e2 ♕c7 12 g4 ♖e8 13 g5 ♘d7

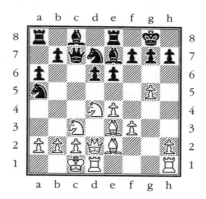

14 g6!

The French press praised White's attacking skill – which is fair enough – but Apicella is only following Tal's example. As we saw in the previous game this is a great way of opening lines against the castled king – especially here because 14...fxe6 allows 15 ♘xe6 followed by the powerful entry of the other knight on d5.

14...hxg6 15 h4 ♘e5

Black signals his clear intention to establish a knight on c4. This is sufficient for White to conjure up a dazzling trap – again linked to the inclusion of the king's rook in the onslaught.

16 h5 ♘ac4 17 ♗xc4 ♘xc4

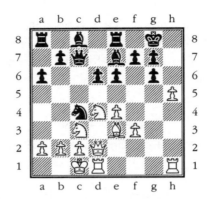

18 hxg6!

A cool move. What does White get for the queen?

18...fxg6

Well, if 18...♘xd2 there is the stunning reply 19 ♖h8+! when White wins after 19...♔xh8 20 gxf7 as the threats of ♖h1 mate and fxe8=♕ are compelling. For example: 20...♕d8 21 ♖h1+ ♗h4 22 ♖xh4+ ♕xh4 23 fxe8=♕+ ♔h7 24 ♔xd2 wins comfortably because the attack continues unabated while Black suffers from a lack of queenside development.

19 ♕g2 ♕b6

You can't blame Collas for cheekily trying to mate in one after he saw the alternative 19...♘xe3 20 ♕xg6 ♗d7 (or 20...♖f8 21 ♖h7 ♗f6 22 ♖dh1 leads to mate) 21 ♘xe6 ♗xe6 22 ♕xe6+ ♔f8 23 ♖h8 mate.

20 ♘a4 ♕d8 21 ♕xg6 ♗f6 22 ♖h7 b5

If the bishop is taken by 22...♘xe3 the attack rages on: 23 ♖g1 (23 ♖dh1? allows Black to struggle on with 23...♔f8) 23...♕e7 – and now that the e7 square is blocked White can think about checkmating on the h-file by 24 ♖gh1.

23 ♖dh1 1-0

When to accept a sacrifice

I'm afraid there are no hard and fast rules telling you when or when not to accept a sacrifice – but I can give you some general pointers. However you should not take the soundness of any sacrifice on trust but work out the consequences as best as you can and make a considered decision. Always bear in mind that a sacrifice might be the result of mistaken calculation or even sheer bluff.

General rules

1   If you are in danger of coming under increased attack by declining a piece sacrifice then provided you cannot see a refutation – take it.

2   If accepting a pawn sacrifice would leave one of your pieces trapped or out of action for a long time – decline it. Only if you can see a clearly favourable outcome should you take the pawn.

3 If a pawn on offer allows your opponent to mobilise his men quickly then provided you can see a way to develop and castle – capture it.

4 If you can win the exchange *(rook for bishop or knight)* **then accept it unless it places your own king in danger or if the rook is poorly placed or if you need to retain your piece for a successful attack.**

It is not easy to make the right choice but if you are in unfamiliar territory, weigh up the consequences carefully before coming to a decision.

The following position – reached after 1 d4 g6 2 ♘f3 ♗g7 3 ♗g5 d6 4 e4 c5 5 c3 ♕b6 6 ♘bd2 – illustrates some of the potential dangers:

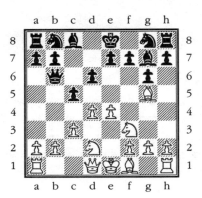

Black has to decide whether he can afford to grab the pawn. He knows that White will then be able to develop his pieces with gain of time by chasing the enemy queen – but he might be able to live with that provided his queen does not get trapped...

6...♕xb2?? 7 ♘c4

White attacks the queen and offers to shed another pawn, which is what Black obviously missed.

7...♕xc3+

Instead 7...♕b5 – to escape the attentions of the knight – is met by 8 ♘xd6+ exd6 9 ♗xb5+ winning the queen by a discovered attack.

8 &d2

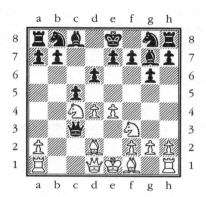

And Black's queen has no safe square to go to!

The general rules can be seen to apply in the following game:

Spraggett – Komljenovic
Seville 2007

1 e4 c5 2 ♘f3 d6 3 d4 cxd4 4 ♘xd4 ♘f6 5 ♘c3 a6

The Najdorf Variation has always been a favourite of the top players – including world champions Bobby Fischer and Garry Kasparov.

6 ♗g5 e6 7 f4 ♕b6 8 ♕d2

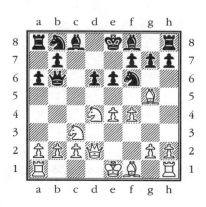

8...♛xb2

Black accepts the offer of the so-called 'Poisoned Pawn' in the hope of hanging on to his extra material. Meanwhile White is counting on excluding the black queen from action for a long time to come. There is still plenty of debate about who is better but in practical terms White often comes out on top because a successful defence demands a very precise knowledge of specific variations.

9 ♘b3

The knight protects the rook and cuts off the queen's retreat along the b-file. Another line is 9 ♖b1.

9...♘bd7

Instead 9...♛a3 was Fischer's choice in his world championship match against Spassky in 1972.

10 ♗xf6 gxf6 11 ♖b1

The queen is ousted before White gets the rest of his pieces into play. He could also develop his kingside along the lines of the main game by 11 ♗e2 ♘c5 12 0-0 (all part of White's plan to increase his attacking options – he ensures there is no threat of ...♘xb3 followed by ...♛xa1) 12...♗d7 13 ♖ab1 ♘xb3? (13...♛a3 is essential but in such positions it is easy to go wrong) 14 axb3 ♛a3 15 b4! (this is what Black missed because now the queen is trapped) 15...♖c8 16 ♖b3 1-0 Luther-Kersten, Bad Zwesten 2002.

11...♛a3 12 ♗e2

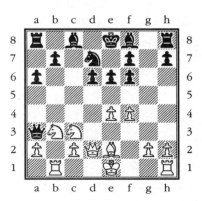

Spraggett has played aggressively but now reverts to general opening principles by completing his development and castling.

12...b5 13 0-0 ♗b7 14 f5

Trying to weaken Black's pawn shield so he can attack the king – which has been detained in the centre.

14...♖c8

It might be wiser to prevent White's next move by playing 14...h5. The game Luther-Vouldis, Bled 2002, continued: 15 fxe6 fxe6 16 ♕e3 ♖c8 17 ♕a7 ♖xc3 18 ♕xb7 ♖xc2 19 ♗d3 ♖c3 20 e5! d5 (or 20...♖xd3 21 ♕c8+ ♔e7 22 exf6+ ♘xf6 23 ♖bc1 threatening ♖c7+ wins) 21 ♗g6+ ♔d8 22 ♖fc1 (the attack works well due to Black's weak defence – a result of his backward development) 22...♖c4 23 ♖xc4 bxc4 24 ♕a8+ ♔c7 25 ♘d4 fxe5 26 ♖b7+ ♔d6 27 ♘b5+! 1-0.

15 ♗h5

Black now has to deal with the threat of 16 fxe6 exploiting the pinned f-pawn.

15...♔e7 16 ♖bd1

The d6 pawn is now reliant on protection from the black queen.

16...♘e5 17 fxe6 fxe6

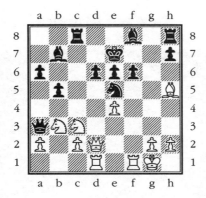

18 ♘b1!

The knight goes back to its starting square to deflect the queen away from defence of the d6 pawn. Such a surprising retreat is easy for Black to miss.

18...♘c4

The black knight comes to the rescue but this only prompts White to make a sensational queen manoeuvre.

19 ♕f2 ♕b2

Black has managed to wriggle out of the immediate danger of losing the d6 pawn and defend against ♕xf6 – but now White can exploit his lead in development.

20 ♕a7 ♖c7 21 ♕b8!

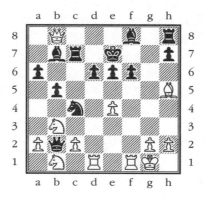

1-0

Black resigned as he is faced with the double threat of ♕e8 mate and the capture of his rook.

How not to attack

9007

We must not forget those players who practice oddball openings and then adopt caveman tactics by going for an all-out attack. The right way to deal with such characters is to fend off their premature attacks, curb their initiative and launch a counterattack. Sounds easy doesn't it? And sometimes it *is* easy – as in the next game.

Richardson – Nakamura
Bermuda 2002

1 e4 c5 2 d4 cxd4 3 ♕xd4?!

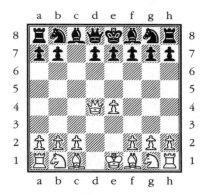

This is risky because the queen can be attacked by Black's minor pieces – thereby giving him an advantage in development. You could argue that Black has been subjected to the element of surprise – but it is a pleasant one! Actually the Morra Gambit – 3 c3 – is a better choice since 3...dxc3 4 ♘xc3 offers White attacking chances thanks to his lead in development and use of the semi-open d-file which can be occupied by a rook.

3...♘c6 4 ♕d1 ♘f6 5 ♘c3 g6

Black responds to White's unusual queen sortie with a cool adherence to the opening principle: *develop and castle*.

6 ♗e3 ♗g7 7 ♗c4 0-0

Nakamura is a top American grandmaster and his robust approach to White's queen sortie is worth noting.

8 h4

This is the sort of wild attack that can produce a quick win – but not against an astute defender who is not fazed by his opponent's obvious intention to open the h-file for his rook. 8 ♘ge2 is met by 8...♘g4 with an edge for Black so 8 h3 is probably a better idea – not particularly inviting when you declared your spirit of adventure on move three.

8...h5

A no-nonsense reply which halts the advance of the h-pawn.

9 ♕d2 ♘e5 10 ♗b3 d6 11 ♘f3 ♘eg4

Though 11...♘xf3+ 12 gxf3 saddles White with doubled pawns it also provides him with the open g-file for his rooks. Richardson has already announced his intention to attack and it would be very provocative indeed to encourage him further.

12 ♗g5 b5!

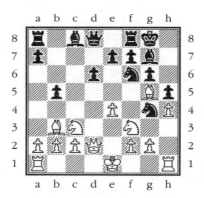

Nakamura knows that White wants to castle queenside and so seizes the opportunity to grab the initiative. The threat is ...b5-b4 removing the defender of the e4 pawn.

13 ♘h2?!

Well, you have to applaud White for his consistency in trying to find ways of complicating matters on the kingside – but this looks horrible. He should not have strayed so far from general opening principles but played 13 0-0-0 (if 13 ♘xb5 then 13...♘xe4 14 ♕d5 ♕a5+! 15 c3 ♘gxf2 with a clear advantage) 13...b4?! (this no longer works well for Black because the queen's rook is much better placed on d1 – however 13...♗b7 is an obvious improvement when Black retains the initiative thanks to his play against the e4 pawn) 14 ♘d5 ♘xe4? 15 ♘xe7+ ♕xe7 16 ♗xe7 ♘xd2 17 ♖xd2 and White is better.

13...b4 14 ♘d5 ♘xh2

I think Black can get away with the startling 14...♘xe4! because 15 ♘xe7+ allows 15...♕xe7! 16 ♗xe7 ♘xd2 17 ♗xf8 (or 17 ♔xd2 ♖e8 18 ♖ae1 ♗xb2 with by far the better chances) 17...♘xb3 18 axb3 ♗xb2 19 ♖b1 ♗c3+ 20 ♔e2 ♔xf8 winning comfortably.

15 ♖xh2 ♘xd5

15...♘xe4 might best be met by 16 ♕e3 when Black has to cope with complications. But not 16 ♘xe7+ ♔h7 17 ♕e3 ♘xg5 18 ♕xg5 ♖e8 winning for Black.

16 ♕xd5 ♗xb2 17 ♖d1

After 17 ♕xa8 Black has no need to take on a1 because the white king is rather vulnerable due to the bad co-ordination of the white pieces. For instance: 17...♗c3+ 18 ♗d2 ♗xd2+ 19 ♔xd2 ♕b6 20 ♕d5 (20 ♖f1 ♕d4+ 21 ♔e1 ♕c3+ 22 ♔d1 ♕a1+ 23 ♔e2 ♗a6+ and wins) 20...♕xf2+ 21 ♔c1 ♕g1+ wins back the rook with a few pawns interest.

17...♗c3+

Black now makes sure the job of winning is quickly done.

18 ♔f1

It is not a good sign that the king has to move like this – but 18 ♗d2 is of little help in view of 18...♗g4 19 f3 ♕b6! threatening ...♕g1+ and ...♕e3 with a terrific position.

18...♕c7 19 ♕d3 a5

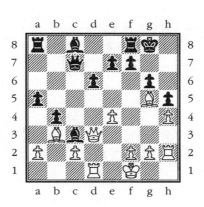

20 f4?

In what is admittedly a bad position White fails to cope with the pressure and makes it easy for Black.

20...♗a6

Win by pin. The queen is lost.

0-1

Develop and castle

Developing your pieces quickly and castling your king into safety sounds easy – but it is so often neglected at every level. This might be due to the difficulty in striking a balance between grabbing a hot pawn and getting the pieces into action. Then again there are plenty of people who simply never get around to castling – a chess sin which can have dire consequences:

Bartel – Fluvia Poyatos
Illes Medes 2007

1 e4 c5 2 ♘f3 ♘c6 3 ♘c3

White declines the invitation to play a standard open Sicilian with 3 d4 and instead brings out the queen's knight to keep Black guessing. Basically it is a move-order trick, hoping that Black will play an inappropriate pawn move before White transposes back into the open Sicilian with 4 d4.

3...♘f6 4 ♗b5

Bartel is still side-stepping the main lines – probably because he wants to avoid the highly tactical Sveshnikov variation which would arise after 4 d4 cxd4 5 ♘xd4 e5.

4...♕c7

Black is ready to take back with the queen if White exchanges pieces on c6. 4...a6 is the obvious move if Black is prepared to accept doubled pawns in order to deprive White of the bishop pair. However White might take on c6 anyway so really there is no need to waste a move encouraging him. For example: 5 ♗xc6 dxc6 6 d3 ♗g4 7 h3 ♗xf3 8 ♕xf3 e6 9 ♗f4 ♗e7 10 0-0-0 (White is able to develop his pieces easily, whereas Black remains rather passive) 10...♘d7 11 d4 cxd4 12 ♖xd4 ♕a5 (Of course 12...e5 fails simply to 13 ♗xe5 taking advantage of the pin on the d-file) 13 ♖hd1 ♖d8 (maybe 13...0-0-0 should be considered.) 14 ♕d3 (White certainly has pressure on the d-file – and it is sufficient to make Black crack) 14...♘c5 15 ♖xd8+ ♗xd8 (or 15...♕xd8 16 ♕g3 wins) 16 ♕d6 f6 17 ♗e3 1-0 Golubev-Guilbert, Bethune 2002.

5 0-0 ♘d4 6 ♖e1 a6

Pushing back the bishop. Instead 6...♘xb5 would allow White a slight initiative as he gains time attacking the black queen. For example: 7 ♘xb5 ♕b6 8 c4! (supporting the knight and helping to control the potentially important d5 square) 8...d6 (if 8...a6 then 9 ♘c3 intending d4 is good because the black queen is misplaced) 9 d4 cxd4 10 e5 dxe5 11 ♘xe5 e6 12 ♕a4! (White now threatens to move the knight and give a discovered check) 12...♗d7 13 ♘xd7 ♘xd7 14 ♗f4 ♖c8 15 ♖ad1 led to an advantage for White in Georgiev-Godard, Agneaux 1998.

7 ♗c4 e6?!

This attempt to reduce the influence of the bishop on the a2-g8 diagonal allows White to take the initiative. Preferable was 7...d6 when 8 ♘d5, 8 e5 and even 8 h3 (to stop the black bishop coming to g4) have all been tried.

8 e5 ♘g4

8...d5 has been mentioned as a possible improvement but after 9 exf6 dxc4 10 ♘xd4 cxd4 11 ♘d5! ♕d6 12 ♕f3 the threat of d2-d3 and ♗f4 causes Black considerable concern.

9 ♘xd4 ♘xe5?!

By grabbing this hot pawn, Black is violating the *develop and castle* principle. He may get away with it – if he has enough time to get his pieces out – but it is a risky business. Also possible is 9...cxd4 10 ♕xg4 ♕xc4 11 d3 (this is the sort of move that is easily missed – White resists the temptation to move the attacked piece and instead frees the way for his bishop with gain of time) 11...♕c5 12 ♘e4 ♕xc2 (12...♕xe5 is not much better in view of the combination 13 ♗f4 ♕d5 14 ♗h6! ♖g8 15 ♘f6+ winning) 13 ♘d6+ ♗xd6 14 exd6 gives White good play because the obvious 14...0-0 is crushed by 15 ♗h6.

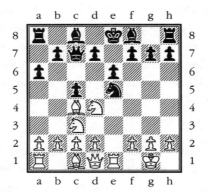

10 ♘f5!

White is temporarily a piece up so can play extravagantly and make good use of his strong rook on the e-file.

10...♘xc4

Black's position collapses after 10...exf5 11 ♘d5 ♕d6 12 d4 cxd4 13 f4.

11 ♕g4

The queen enters the fray with an attack on both the knight on c4 and pawn on g7. Black's defence looks bleak with his king stuck in the middle and only two pieces developed.

11...♘e5 12 ♘xg7+ ♗xg7 13 ♕xg7 ♘g6 14 d4

The game might be equal on pawns and pieces but White is clearly winning on position. In particular he can exploit the weak dark squares around the black king.

14...cxd4 15 ♘d5 ♛c5 16 ♖e5

A crafty move which threatens the discovered attack ♘f6+ winning the black queen.

16...♛f8 17 ♛f6

There is no question of exchanging queens into an endgame – Bartel is playing for checkmate.

17...d6 18 ♖e1

Simple and strong – once again there is an imminent threat of ♘c7+.

18...♖b8 19 ♛xd4 b6 20 ♛c3 ♗d7

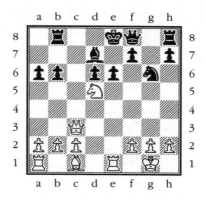

21 ♗g5 1-0

Black resigned due to the threat of 22 ♘c7 mate. His brittle defence can offer no more resistance: 21...♖c8 22 ♛d2 ♗c6 23 ♘f6+ ♚d8 24 ♘xh7+ wins the queen and 21...♗b5 22 ♛c7 threatening ♘f6 mate and ♛xb8 is decisive.

In the next game the strongest woman player in the world Judit Polgar plays actively and manages to force a concession in the opening in that White is obliged to move his king – thus forfeiting the right to castle. This is enough for Judit to give a master class on how to exploit such an advantage in the most incisive fashion:

Van Wely – J. Polgar
Wijk aan Zee 1997

1 c4

White plays the English opening, which has a reputation for being safe and reliable.

1...c5 2 ♘c3 ♘c6 3 e3 ♘f6 4 d4 d5 5 dxc5

This is only a temporary win of a pawn but after it is recaptured White gains time with a queenside pawn advance.

5...e6 6 a3 ♗xc5 7 b4 ♗d6 8 ♘f3

At first sight it appears that White can win a pawn but that is not so: 8 cxd5 exd5 9 ♘xd5? ♘xd5 10 ♕xd5? ♗xb4+ and the discovered attack on the queen wins.

8...0-0 9 cxd5 exd5

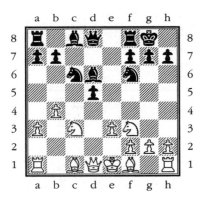

White has achieved a principal objective: Black has been saddled with an *isolated pawn* – so called because it has no friendly pawn on either side to protect it. The long-term plan is to undermine and attack it and use the square in front of it – d4 – as an outpost for his pieces. However Black too has access to some good squares – notably e4 and c4.

10 ♘b5?!

An elaborate manoeuvre which threatens to exchange knight for bishop and gain superiority on the dark squares – with the bishop on b2 playing a major role on the long diagonal. However it would be simpler to play 10 &e2 followed by 11 0-0 before embarking on queenside play.

10...&b8 11 &b2

After placing the d5 pawn under surveillance White now introduces a latent threat to remove its bodyguard on f6.

11...a5!

Polgar finds an active continuation which undermines White's pawn structure and brings the queen's rook to life.

12 bxa5

White has little choice but to take the pawn because the alternatives are fine for Black.

12 &xf6 is premature because after 12...&xf6 the d5 pawn cannot be taken due to the unprotected rook on a1. And 13 bxa5 &f5 14 &c1 &xa5 leaves Black with the better chances. Also possible is 12 &e2 axb4 13 axb4 &xa1 14 &xa1 &xb4 (Black is a pawn up and although White could argue that he has some compensation because of his control of the a1-h8 diagonal – it is not enough) 15 0-0 &f5 with an edge.

12...&e4!

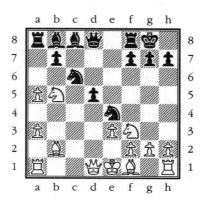

A clever idea which prepares to take on a5 with the queen and exploit the fact that the white king is still on its original square.

13 &e2 &xa5+ 14 &f1

This already breaks the general rule of *develop and castle* so is not a good sign for White. And blocking the check by 14 &d2 leaves White suffering after 14...♖e8 (perhaps the line 14...♘e5 15 f3 ♘c4 16 ♗xc4 dxc4 is worth investigating) 15 f3 (otherwise White is tied to the defence of d2 which puts him in a stranglehold) 15...♘xd2 16 ♕xd2 ♖xe3! winning.

14...♖d8 15 h3

White now has to waste time castling artificially so as to be able to connect his rooks. Of course an immediate 15 g3 is no good because of 15...♗h3+ containing the king – so Black has to be denied that move.

15...♕b6

An important idea. Most players would just leave the queen on a5 until something turned up. Instead Polgar demonstrates her class by dropping the queen back in readiness for its transfer to the kingside.

16 g3 ♖e8 17 ♕e1 ♘a5

The knight not only heads for the aggressive c4 square but clears the sixth rank for the passage of the black queen.

18 ♗d4 ♕g6 19 ♔g2

It has taken some time for White to get his pieces co-ordinated – and in the meantime Black has built up a formidable attack.

19...♘c4 20 ♘h4 ♕c6 21 a4 ♖a6 22 ♗g4 f5!?

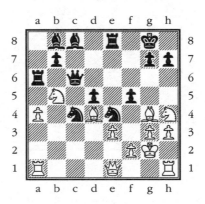

An inspired pawn sacrifice to open the f-file for the king's rook and bolster the attack against the white king.

23 ♗xf5

If the pawn is not taken then Judit will further advance her kingside pawns and expose the white king.

For example:

a) 23 ♗f3 allows 23...g5 trapping the knight.

b) 23 ♗e2 g5 24 ♘f3 f4 and White's pawn cover will be broken up.

c) 23 ♘xf5 and now Black has a pleasant choice:

c1) 23...♗xf5 24 ♗xf5 ♘xg3! (a clever combination that works well thanks to some neat tactics) 25 fxg3 ♘xe3+ 26 ♗xe3 d4+ 27 ♔h2 ♖xe3 28 ♘xd4 ♖xe1 29 ♘xc6 ♖e2+ 30 ♔g1 ♖xc6 31 ♔f1 ♖b2 with a superior endgame.

c2) 23...h5 24 ♘xg7 hxg4 25 hxg4 ♖f8! 26 ♖a2 (or 26 ♘f5 ♗xf5 27 gxf5 ♘e5 and Black is on top) 26...♗xg4 with a big advantage.

23...♖f8 24 ♗xc8?!

It might be better to exchange the well placed knight with 24 ♗xe4 when good chances are offered by 24...dxe4 25 ♕b4 ♕e6 followed by ...♘e5 and ...g5-g4 as in the main game.

24...♕xc8 25 ♖a2 ♖h6

The rook is well placed to exert pressure on the h3 pawn and to oust the knight on h4 by ...g5.

26 ♕d1

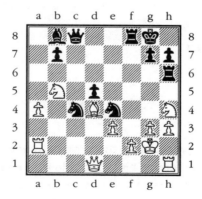

26...g5

This goes against the maxim *do not expose your king* but in the present circumstances it is very effective. This is partly because the centre is closed

– making it difficult for White to launch a quick attack – and of course because Black's pieces are well placed for the onslaught.

27 ♘f3 g4 28 hxg4

If White retreats the knight by 28 ♘g1 then 28...gxh3+! plunges White into deep trouble: 29 ♖xh3 (alternatively, 29 ♘xh3 fails to 29...♖xh3! 30 ♖xh3 ♖xf2+ 31 ♖xf2 ♕xh3+! 32 ♔xh3 ♘xf2+ 33 ♔g2 ♘xd1 leading to a winning material advantage) 29...♘xf2! 30 ♖xf2 ♖xf2+ 31 ♔xf2 ♖xh3 32 ♘xh3 ♕xh3 wins.

28...♖xh1 29 ♕xh1 ♕xg4

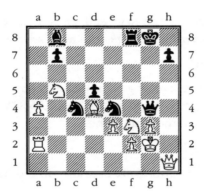

Black is now threatening to take the knight on f3 as well as to strip the castled king bare by 30...♗xg3.

30 ♘h2 ♖xf2+! 0-1

Fighting chess

Garry Kasparov is undoubtedly the most advanced chess player of all time and successfully defended his world title five times during his 15 year reign. His style is difficult to imitate because he is such a versatile all-round player – but his games are always characterised by immense energy. He retired prematurely from top level chess in his early 40s whilst still rated No. 1 in the world and entered the dangerous world of Russian politics.

After his official retirement he only took part in one tournament – a blitz event from which we take the following game.

Kasparov – Korchnoi
Zurich 2006

1 d4 ♘f6 2 c4 e6 3 ♘f3 ♗b4+ 4 ♗d2

The standard way to meet the Bogo-Indian. Instead 4 ♘c3 would transpose to the Nimzo-Indian, while the lesser known 4 ♘bd2 is worth investigating.

4...a5

Black can exchange on d2 immediately but often protects the bishop with this pawn move or by playing his queen to e7. His idea is to keep the opponent guessing about his future plans.

5 ♘c3

After 5 ♗xb4 axb4 Black has a perfectly playable game – his pawn on b4 is safe and his queen's rook can become active on the a-file.

5...b6 6 e3

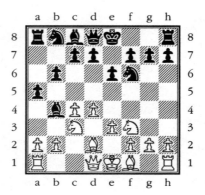

Kasparov now proceeds to complete his kingside development and castle – only then will he embark on a middlegame attack.

6...♗b7 7 ♗d3 0-0

Though 7...♗xc3 is possible – with the idea of taking control of the e4 square and planting a knight there – 8 ♗xc3 ♘e4 9 ♗xe4 ♗xe4 10 d5 f6 11 ♕d4 does favour White. On the other hand 7...d6 8 ♕c2 ♘bd7 9 e4 e5 10 ♘d5! ♗xd2+ 11 ♕xd2 exd4 (or 11...c6 12 ♘c3 0-0 13 0-0 offers a balanced position) 12 ♘xd4 ♘c5 13 0-0 led to equal chances in Kasparov-Tal, Niksic 1983.

8 0-0 d5 9 cxd5 exd5

If 9...♘xd5 then 10 e4 gives White central control and the slightly better game after 10...♘xc3 11 bxc3 ♗e7 12 ♕e2.

10 a3 ♗d6 11 ♘e5

The knight takes up a very strong position in the centre and will be supported by f2-f4 which also opens up new attacking options for White such as ♕f3-h3.

11...c5 12 f4 ♞c6 13 ♞b5

The knight is well placed on b5 where it protects the d4 pawn. And if the bishop takes on e5, the knight on b5 can even look forward to occupying the d6 square. 13 ♛f3 is not so good because of the pressure against the d4 pawn: 13...cxd4 14 ♞xc6 ♝xc6 15 exd4 with a level position.

13...cxd4 14 exd4 ♞e7 15 f5!

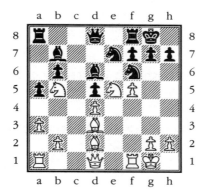

The advance of the f-pawn prevents any emergence of the black knight on g6. It is a particularly unpleasant position for Korchnoi who is under pressure and without counterplay.

15...♞e4 16 ♝xe4 dxe4 17 f6

The exchange of the black knight on f6 enables the f-pawn to find another role. Now Black's castle wall will be seriously damaged.

17...♝xe5

The capture of the pawn leads to loss of material or mate: 17...gxf6 18 ♛g4+ ♚h8 (or 18...♞g6 19 ♞d7! ♝c8 20 ♞xd6 ♝xd7 21 ♛xe4 with a clear advantage) 19 ♝h6 ♞g6 (of course 19...♜g8?? would be disastrous in view of 20 ♞xf7 mate) 20 ♝xf8 winning.

18 dxe5 ♞g6 19 fxg7

Now White can get at the exposed enemy king.

19...♚xg7 20 ♞d6 ♝a6

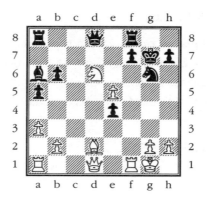

21 ♗h6+!

A brilliant stroke which highlights the fragility of Black's defence.

21...♔g8

The alternative is to walk the plank – 21...♔xh6 22 ♘f5+ ♔g5 23 ♕c1+ ♔h5 24 ♕h6+ ♔g4 25 h3 mate.

22 ♖f5

Kasparov can take the rook whenever he wants because it dare not move. Therefore he improves the position of his own rook before thinking about any gain of material.

22...♕h4?

An abrupt end. In a desperate situation the queen commits suicide.

23 ♗g5 1-0

The queen has no safe escape squares.

Predict-a-move

It is natural that attacking positions reap the greatest benefit from the *predict-a-move* method as they provide fertile ground for setting traps against obvious replies:

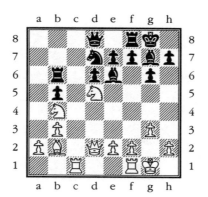

Vladimirov – Marrero
Groningen 1976

Black meets White's 17 ♘cd5 with a reflex action exchange of the dark squared bishops: **17...♗xb2?** and is stunned by **18 ♖c8!** after which 18...♕xc8 19 ♘xe7+ wins the queen by a knight fork.

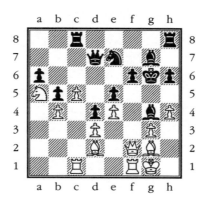

Miezis – Lelumees
Tallinn 2007

After **29 c6** Black can see nothing wrong with grabbing the dangerous-looking passed c-pawn. **29...♘xc6?** He should play 29...♕e6. **30 ♘xc6 ♖xc6 31 ♖xc6 ♕xc6** But now after the forced exchanges we see why White was so keen on all those exchanges on c6...

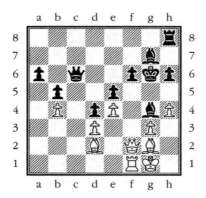

32 ♕f5+! A big shock. White's king's bishop suddenly springs to life after 32...♗xf5 33 exf5+ ♔f7 34 ♗xc6 and White emerges a piece up. **1-0**

In the heat of battle there will always be opportunities to catch out the opponent with some trap or other. But you must always remember to mobilise your forces beforehand so you have a sufficient number of combat-ready pieces to achieve your objectives.

Day 5
Avoiding blunders

Chess Trivia — After the success of a number of hand-written volumes on the royal game, the first printed chess book was released in 1475. It was called 'The Game and Playe of the Chess'.

In such a complex game as chess it is inevitable that you will make mistakes. However you can cut down on errors by following these rules:

Rules

1 Look for simple threats.

Do not become so engrossed in your deep plans that you overlook simple traps laid by your opponent – for example the kind set by the *predict-a-move* method. Even grandmasters stumble – so remain in a state of high alert to checks and threats.

2 Search for forced moves.

A forcing sequence of moves can lead you unwittingly into a position where you get stung by some tactic that has been cunningly prepared by your opponent. So before thinking about what *you* want to do, take a quick look around and see what *your opponent* is up to. Give priority to potential mating threats, checks and captures.

3 Avoid time-trouble.

You have only yourself to blame if you blunder because of time pressure. So take steps to improve your handling of the clock. For example, a good knowledge of your favourite openings will save you a great deal of time in the early part of the game.

I recall English grandmaster William Watson regularly spending twenty minutes or so before making even his first move! He was probably contemplating the best plan of campaign against that particular opponent. A grand gesture perhaps – but it inevitably led to time-trouble and mixed results.

Be practical – not theatrical. When there is only one sensible move, don't think about it – just play it! If your opponent plays queen takes queen check and the only option is king takes queen – don't spend five minutes gazing serenely at the other boards before recapturing.

4 Catch up on development.

Trying to cope with surprise moves in the opening is a common cause of blunders – so you have to be extra careful. Never forget the golden rule of *develop and castle* which will help you to avoid those stressful situations that can induce mistakes.

5 Take it easy.

Don't rush to make your move without first trying to find out what your opponent has up his sleeve. It is not unusual for a player to calculate a long variation, find something wrong with it after 15 minutes and then decide to play something else in a matter of 30 seconds. If this sounds familiar – calmly go through the rules again and you will probably avoid any obvious mistakes.

Time trouble

Your opponent is in time-trouble

Again and again you see players, with plenty of time left on their clock, suddenly start to play quickly in an endeavour to hustle their opponent who *is* in time-trouble. Yes – it does sometimes work but unless you have a completely lost position why rush and run a greater risk of making a mistake?

Here are two consecutive rounds from the World Junior Championship in Armenia 2006 where the Australian Tomek Rej tries to take advantage of his opponent's time-trouble.

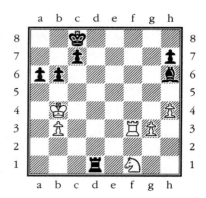

Hungaski – Rej
World Junior Championship 2006

Black can eradicate any danger of a swindle by calmly playing **38...♗g7!!** which traps the enemy king and weaves a mating net.

For example:

a) 39 ♘h2 ♗b2 (with the threat of 40...♖d4 mate) 40 ♖f4 ♖c1 41 ♖c4 c5+ 42 ♔a4 ♖a1 mate.

b) 39 ♖f2 c5+ 40 ♔c4 (or 40 ♔a3 ♖a1+ 41 ♖a2 ♖xf1 winning thanks to the extra piece) 40...b5+ 41 ♔xc5 ♗d4+) 39...♗b2 40 ♖f4 ♖c1 41 ♖c4 c5+ 42 ♔a4 ♖a1 mate.

Instead Black played the cautious **38...♖d7** and White wriggled out of trouble: **39 ♔c3 c5 40 ♔c2 ♔c7 41 g4 ♗g7 42 g5 ♔d6 43 ♘g3 ♔e6 44 ♘f5** with a draw agreed after another 20 moves.

Though they say lightning doesn't strike twice, I think Rej should avoid stormy weather because the next day he missed another checkmate – again when it was his opponent who was in time-trouble!

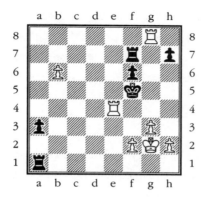

Rej – Brandenburg
World Junior Championship 2006

In this position, against a Dutch player, Rej can clinch victory by **37 ♔f3!** which threatens 38 g4 mate – or a delayed version of it after 37...h5 38 h3. Instead there followed: **37 ♖b4? a2 38 ♖a8 ♖b7 39 ♖b2 ♔g6 40 ♔f3 ♖b1 41 ♖axa2 ♖xb6 42 ♖xb1 ♖xb1 43 ♔g4** and the game was eventually drawn in 64 moves.

I can also remember a game where my opponent, an Israeli grandmaster, was playing so fast in order to capitalise on my time-trouble that he went horribly wrong:

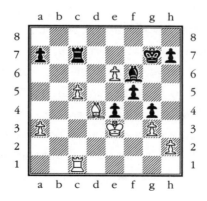

Murey – Lane
Manchester 1983

I played **30...♔g6** to *unpin* the bishop and ease my way to a draw. But back came **31 c6??** to which I replied **31...♗g5+** The *skewer!* White's rook will be captured next move. My opponent missed this simple tactic by playing so fast that he forgot that my bishop was no longer pinned.

These examples show the very real dangers of rushing your moves in the hope that your opponent will lose on time. Think about it. He has only two minutes – you all the time in the world. Yet you are now effectively playing with the same amount of time as him – and you can easily go wrong. It is a much better idea to take your time to find a decent plan or use the *predict-a-move* method to calculate a combination and let your stressed opponent play the obvious moves and lose.

There is nothing new in all this as you can see from this extract from the book *Chess Treasury of the Air* where Bob Wade writes "I remember playing the German master Sämisch in a tournament in Germany in 1949. After 22 moves he had used up so much time that he had only two minutes left for his next 18 – which he was capable of in his tensed-up state, amid the excitement of craning spectators. I viewed the difficult position (and the spectators) sourly; but I noted that I had an hour and a half for my own moves. My reaction? I ordered tea, waited till it came (while my clock ticked), slowly stirred it and drank it, and slowly pondered; and did not move for an hour. The frustrated spectators had long before moved on to more exciting games. My opponent could not stay at the pitch of intensity to which he had raised himself an hour before; his thinking slowed and wandered, and he became visibly relaxed. After I had moved, he actually only made a couple of moves before overstepping the time, and thus losing. I had learnt a valuable lesson."

So next time you find yourself in this sort of situation, follow Bob Wade's example – even if you do order a capuccino instead.

I am in time-trouble

But it's better you weren't! So try to ensure it happens as infrequently as possible. On the other hand if you are a time trouble addict you are probably already used to the vultures that gather around your board. Those spectators are enjoying every moment of your panic-ridden predicament! And in the long-term this state of affairs will not do you or your chess any good. However, knowing how hard it is to kick the time trouble habit I can at least offer you the following tips:

I Always have a safe move available.

This is useful if the other player is playing it cool and just improving the positions of his pieces without any obvious threats.

2 Spot the tactic.

Your opponent may well be tempted to try a blatant trick or two – so remain on red alert!

3 Find a plan.

If you get the chance, use your *opponent's* time to devise a constructive plan.

You might also use psychology. For example, if you have the worse position then why not offer a draw? Though it may be rejected it does usually make the player with more time stop and think. Should he accept it or not accept it? All of which can gain you valuable thinking time.

But just in case you are still optimistic about surviving time scrambles here is a reminder of what to expect:

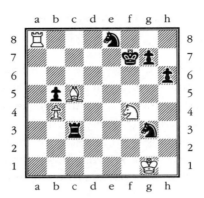

Trent – Emms
Southend 2006

Black is two pawns ahead but has practically no time left and blundered spectacularly with **45...♘f6??** allowing **46 ♖f8 mate**.

One typical time-trouble mistake is to assume that when you attack a piece it will move – and then you start to calculate what you are going to do on the second move... A sure way of missing something else!

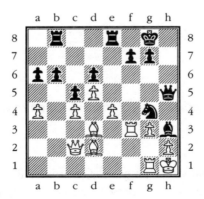

Chabannon – Bauer
French Championship 1997

White is worrying himself over a move by the black bishop followed by ♛xh2 mate. So he played **32 ♖f5??** attacking the queen. However he overlooked **32...♛xf5!** and instead of the queen delivering a checkmate, the black knight has this privilege – 33 exf5 ♘f2 mate. **0-1**

A special case

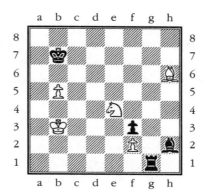

Howell – Ward
Gausdal 2005

Here we have a classic situation where White has no winning chances – apart from one very faint hope... And indeed after careful consideration of the pros and cons of the position and a measured look at various endgame scenarios, *Black lost on time!*

What happened? Well, this is a special case where a player has failed to write down his moves correctly. In my experience of coaching juniors and improving players, an error in writing down the moves usually occurs when things become complicated, such as when a player is faced with an unusual opening. A couple of moves are missed out or White writes down his move where Black's should be – it's all very careless. There is a school of thought that says "Just get on with it – make one extra move at the end of the time-control." But, as shown by the example in Chapter One, I did this and blundered into a mate in one!

So get into the good habit of handling your scoresheet properly – it will avoid upsets and reward you with a win every now and then that you might otherwise not have achieved. You need all the help you can get when plunged into time-trouble – and knowing how many moves you have to make is absolutely vital.

I am too good to make a mistake

If you think your play is perfect — then dream on. Everybody makes mistakes, even world champions, so keep alert from the first move to the last.

Let's look at a bad experience of former US champion Joel Benjamin which shows how even the best intentions can end in disaster when a player moves too quickly or loses his sense of danger:

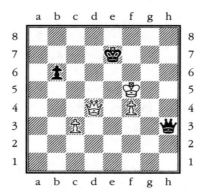

Benjamin — Gufeld
Honolulu 1998

The spectators could see that the extra pawn gives White winning chances but few could have predicted Benjamin's move **80 ♔e5??** which allowed the shock **80...♛e6 mate**.

Blunder of the century

Vladimir Kramnik had the dubious honour of making the most expensive mistake in chess history. In a match against the computer Deep Fritz the world champion threw away his chance to win the million dollar prize with an appalling blunder.

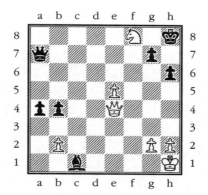

Deep Fritz – Kramnik
Man v machine, Bonn 2006

With plenty of time on the clock Kramnik now played **34...♕e3??** and was so confident that he stood up and proceeded to make his way to the coffee area. At this moment the embarrassed gentleman executing Fritz's moves on the board was panicking because, in front of a live crowd and an Internet audience of hundreds of thousands, there appeared to be a technical hitch. He simply could not believe that the world champion had allowed mate in one! The operator played **35 ♕h7 mate** upon which Kramnik hurried back to the board in a state of shock. Just for the record 34...♔g8 leads to a draw – and I have that on good authority from Deep Fritz itself.

The excuse

At the press conference immediately after the game Kramnik had this to say: "It was actually not only about the last move. I was calculating this line very long in advance, and then recalculating. It was very strange, some kind of blackout. I was feeling well, I was playing well, I think I was pretty much better. I calculated the line many, many times, rechecking myself. I already calculated this line when I played 29...♕a7, and after each move I was recalculating, again, and again, and finally blundered mate in one. Actually, it was the first time that it happened to me, and I cannot find any explanation. I was not feeling tired, I think I was calculating well during the whole game. It is just very strange, I cannot explain it."

Translation: "I missed it."

Winning moves

The ultimate mistake is to allow checkmate – but *blundering material* is far more frequently seen:

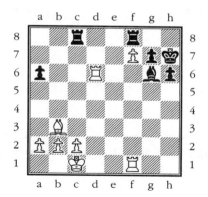

Handke – Pelletier
German Team Championship 2002

White is ahead on material but gets carried away with **40 ♖xa6?** which allows the crushing **40...♗d3** and Black wins a rook. How could a grandmaster miss such a move? Well, the only rational explanation is that he forgot the c-pawn was pinned by the rook on c8.

Hard to believe? Perhaps, but even world champions can have blackouts.

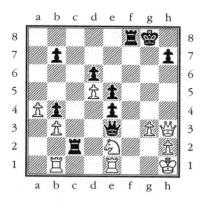

Keene – Botvinnik
Hastings 1966/67

In this position the maestro playing Black could not resist **34...♖xe2?** – thereby missing **35 ♕g4+** winning material. Keene commented "at which point Botvinnik gasped, raised his hand to his forehead and resigned." In fact 34...♖f2 would have led to a draw because 35 ♕e6+ ♔g7 36 ♕d7+ is a perpetual check.

Predict-a-move

A theme that I have already explored is how it is possible to predict the opponent's move and take advantage of it by setting a trap. Take this position:

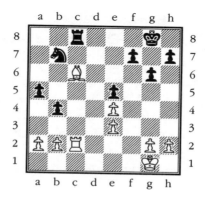

Li Shilong – Wang Yue
Wuxi 2006

Black has just moved his knight from d6 to b7. At this point White, no mean player, noted that 33...♘d8 does not win the 'pinned' bishop because it can safely retreat to a4 where it will protect the rook. Therefore White casually played **33 ♔f2??** whereupon his position collapsed after **33...b3!** which blocks the a4-d1 diagonal and invalidates White's planned defence. Play continued **34 axb3** White has no choice because if 34 ♖c1 then simply 34...bxa2 threatening ...♖xc6 on the next move – since rook takes rook allows the pawn to queen. **34...♘d8** Now 35 ♗a4 no longer protects the rook because the pawn on b3 is in the way – so White must lose a piece. **35 b4 ♖xc6 0-1**

A win or draw so I resign!

I have noticed that when a player has a bad position he often gives up hope and lets the game slip away very quickly. But he should not do that. Even against all the odds there is always a last ditch chance to salvage the game – as we shall see in the chapter on 'swindling'.

By way of example the following position has stuck in my mind for over twenty years – it is a warning to us all:

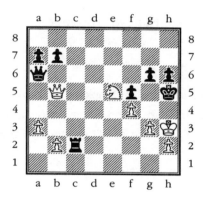

Dekhanov – K. Yusupov
Uzbekistan Championship 1981

At this moment White resigned, thinking that if he avoided an exchange of queens then he would be finished off by ...♕f1 mate. And if he swapped queens he would have no chance in the endgame because of his material deficit. But – miracle of miracles – White could have won with the superb combination **1 g4+!! fxg4 2 ♘xg4+ ♕xb5** (or 2...g5 3 ♕e8+ ♕f7 4 ♘f6 mate) **3 ♘f6 mate**.

So as a general rule: give the position a few minutes thought before you give up hope. After all, if you resign you will have a long wait before the next round – so what difference does a few minutes make? Even if you only discover a saving move once in every fifty games you will still improve your chess awareness and become a far more resourceful player.

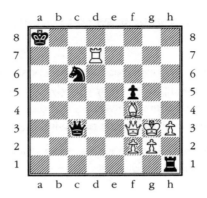

Klinova – Spence
Gibraltar 2006

It is a slight understatement but Black's best move here is *not* to resign as he did in the game. Instead, he could have gloriously saved the day with **42...♕g7+!! 43 ♖xg7** (43 ♔h4 ♕xd7 is winning for Black) **43...♖xh3+! 44 ♔xh3** stalemate.

Take a break

Sometimes you can get confused and muddle up previously planned moves of a combination. It is easy to get carried away in the excitement and be rather pleased with yourself that a combination is going to swing the game in your favour – so much so that you forget to play the moves in the right order! In the old days I would have said "Write down your move before you play it" but the laws of chess have changed and this is now forbidden. Therefore it is best to make a mental note of all the opponent's obvious threats – then reinforce this by reciting your intended replies in your head. Adopting this simple procedure will help you avoid confusion and error.

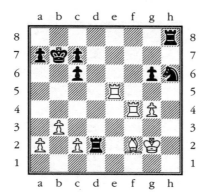

Shaw – S.Williams
British Team Championship (4NCL) 2005

In this position the English international playing Black thought up the crafty idea of **33...♘xg4!** 34 ♖xg4 ♖f8 recovering the piece with good winning chances. So how do you explain **33...♖f8??** transposing the moves of the combination and handing White a win on a plate by **34 ♖xf8**.

Ring, Ring...

If you want to be complete player then you must cover every eventuality – which means learning from the following bad experience:

Winants – Abolianin
Belgian Team Championship 2000

1 d4 g6 2 e4 c6 3 c4 ♗g7 4 ♘c3 d6 5 ♗e3 ♘f6 6 ♗e2 ♘a6 7 f4 ♕a5 8 ♗d2 ♕b6 9 e5 dxe5 10 fxe5 ♘g8 11 ♘f3 ♗g4 12 c5 ♕c7 13 ♕a4

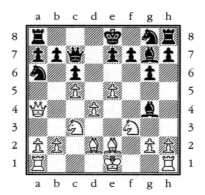

There is no need for us to discuss the respective middlegame chances of the two sides because at this moment *White won*. But how? Well, a little later Luc Winants told me. After leaving the board to buy a cup of coffee he returned to find all the chess pieces had been reset on their original squares and his opponent had disappeared! Astonished, he looked around to see if someone was playing a joke on him – when a team mate whispered the ominous words "his phone rang". Too right. The official rules of chess now state that if your mobile goes off during a game then you lose. And it happens more often than you might think.

Day 6
Mastering the endgame

Chess trivia — The longest game ever in a world championship match was 124 moves between Viktor Korchnoi and Anatoly Karpov in 1978.

The endgame is the final phase of the game where few pieces remain on the board. It can be hard graft studying the endgame because, unlike openings, there are no quick fixes and no instant rewards. Moreover only a relatively small percentage of games actually reach an endgame. No wonder it is so often neglected. Grandmaster David Janowsky even admitted "I detest the endgame!"

It is not realistic to suppose that you will suddenly be prepared to spend a great deal of time studying this part of the game – but as a practical player you will need to have a certain amount of essential knowledge in order to win won endgames and draw drawn ones.

So here are a few guidelines that will enable you to give a good account of yourself in typical endgames where elementary mistakes tend to be repeated over and again.

Basic instincts

The basic checkmates – for example with queen or rook versus king – are pretty straightfoward but there are others where the technique has to be learned. It makes sense to know how to checkmate with only minor pieces on the board because these endgames really do occur in practical play. Then again you need to know the best way to prolong the game if you are on the defending side – because the attacker has only 50 moves to checkmate you otherwise you can claim a draw. By the way, that does not mean 25 moves each by Black and White – which was the view of one recent tournament competitor whose claim for a draw was *not* upheld!

Checkmate with two bishops

General rules

1 The king and two bishops combine to force the defending king to the edge of the board.

2 The defending king is forced into any corner and then checkmated.

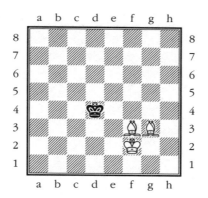

1...♔d3 2 ♗e5 ♔d2 3 ♗e4 ♔c1 The black king is already forced to the edge of the board and now the task is to checkmate in any one of the corners. **4 ♔e3 4** ♔e2?? is stalemate. **4...♔d1 5 ♔d3 ♔e1** After 5...♔c1 White engineers a mate on the a1 square: 6 ♗f3 ♔b1 7 ♔c3 ♔a2 8 ♗d6 ♔b1 9 ♔b3 ♔c1 10 ♗f4+ ♔b1 11 ♗e4+ ♔a1 12 ♗e5 mate. **6 ♗g3+ ♔f1** The king shuffles along the a-file but cannot avoid mate in one of the corners. Or 6...♔d1 7 ♗f3+ ♔c1 8 ♔c3 ♔b1 9 ♔b3 ♔c1 10 ♗f4+ ♔b1 11 ♗e4+ ♔a1 12 ♗e5 mate. **7 ♔e3 ♔g1 8 ♔f3 ♔f1** If 8...♔h1 then 9 ♔f2 mate. **9 ♗d3+ ♔g1 10 ♗f4 ♔h1 11 ♔g3 ♔g1 12 ♗e3+ ♔h1 13 ♗e4 mate.**

Checkmate with two knights

General rules

1 It is not possible to *force* checkmate with a king and two knights.

2 However it would be wrong to say that you cannot checkmate with two knights – it *can* be done but only with your opponent's cooperation!

1 ♘f6+ ♚h8?? Correct is 1...♚f8 and White cannot checkmate because there are always stalemate possibilities. 2 ♘f7 mate.

The exception

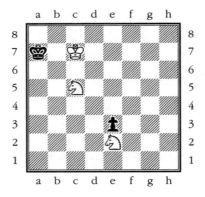

It is strange but true that if the defender has a pawn on the board in the two knights v king endgame it is more likely he will be checkmated. This is because the pawn is blockaded while the attacker is forcing the king into a corner. Only then will the blockade be lifted and the fact that the opponent now has a pawn move kills any chance of stalemate.

1 ♘d4 e2 2 ♘c6+ It should be clear that 2 ♘xe2 would result in a draw. 2...♚a8 3 ♘a4 e1=♕ 4 ♘b6 mate

I once had this endgame at the Hastings tournament – but it is very rare. My opponent seemed to have no knowledge of it at all because he complained to the arbiter that I was carrying on in a drawn position. It took hours to win and this was not helped by an over-zealous organiser who – at one point when both players were away from the board – wrongly assumed that nobody would play on in such a position and promptly put all the pieces back on the original squares ready for the next game!

Bishop and knight versus king

General rules

I The defending king is forced to the side of the board by the opponent's pieces.

2 The defending king is then forced along to the corner of the board *where the colour of the square is the same as the bishop* – to enable checkmate to be delivered.

As the player with the two pieces has only 50 moves to achieve checkmate I would recommend that you keep playing on and on if you are defending with a lone king – because it will be difficult for your opponent to checkmate you if he doesn't know the proper method.

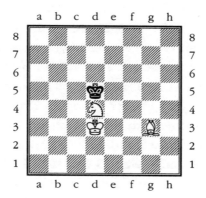

I ♘b3 ♚c6 2 ♚c4 ♚b6 3 ♘c5 ♚c6 4 ♘a4 This idea of moving the knight back in order to force the king to give way is crucial in this endgame. White uses the knight and bishop to cover the squares to the left and right of the king – which is eventually driven back to the edge of the board. **4...♔b7 5 ♔b5 ♔c8 6 ♔c6 ♔d8 7 ♔d6 ♔c8** Heading for the dark-squared corner by 7...♔e8 is what White wants – because that is where checkmate will be delivered, e.g. 8 ♔e6 ♔f8 (or 8...♔d8 9 ♘b6 again ensuring that the king goes to the dark squared corner) 9 ♗e5 ♔e8 10 ♗f6 ♔f8 11 ♘c5 and mate will soon follow. **8 ♘b6+ ♔b7 9 ♔c5 ♔a6 10 ♔c6 ♔a5 11 ♗d6 ♔a6 12 ♗b8** This forces the king out of the wrong corner and along the file towards a1 where the bishop will be able to checkmate. **12...♔a5 13 ♘d5!**

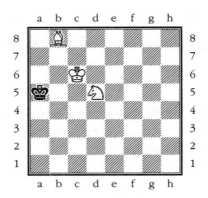

This is the most difficult move to remember – only in this way can you achieve the mating formation. Though the knight appears to allow the black king off the edge, it will soon be driven back again. **13...♔a4** Or 13...♔a6 14 ♘b4+ ♔a5 15 ♔c5 ♔a4 16 ♔c4 ♔a5 17 ♗c7+ ♔a4 18 ♘d3 ♔a3 19 ♗f4 ♔a4 20 ♘c5+ ♔a3 21 ♔c3 and checkmate is imminent. **14 ♔c5 ♔b3 15 ♘b4!** From here the knight prevents the king heading for another corner of the board. **15...♔c3 16 ♗f4** The mating net is almost completed because the bishop cuts off the king's retreat. **16...♔b3 17 ♗e5 ♔a4 18 ♔c4 ♔a5 19 ♗c7+ ♔a4 20 ♘d3 ♔a3 21 ♗b6** White waits for the right moment to finally push the king into the corner. **21...♔a4** Or 21...♔a2 22 ♗c5 ♔b1 23 ♔b3 ♔a1 24 ♔c2 ♔a2 25 ♘c1+ ♔a1 26 ♗d4 mate. **22 ♘b2+ ♔a3 23 ♔c3 ♔a2 24 ♔c2 ♔a3 25 ♗c5+** Now all White's pieces are perfectly placed to give checkmate in the corner that is of the same colour as the bishop. **25...♔a2 26 ♘d3 ♔a1 27 ♗b4 ♔a2 28 ♘c1+ ♔a1 29 ♗c3 mate.**

King and pawn endgames

There are a couple of basic king and pawn endgames that you simply *must* know. They can also help you to understand more complicated versions on the same theme.

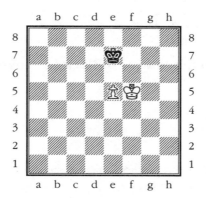

This position occurs frequently in international competitions yet players can still get it wrong. It should be a draw irrespective of whether it is

White or Black to move. Players who do not have knowledge of the defensive method often assume that White will win because of his extra pawn – but this is not the case.

I e6 ♚e8 The only move. When the attacking king advances you must be able *to move to a square directly opposite it*. So not 1...♚f8?? 2 ♚f6 ♚e8 (now – compared to the main line – Black has to give way and can longer achieve stalemate) 3 e7 ♚d7 4 ♚f7 winning. **2 ♚f6** If White tries to be clever with 2 ♚e5 then 2...♚e7 is correct when 3 ♚d5 is met by 3...♚e8! preparing to face the king after 4 ♚d6 ♚d8 whereupon the game will finish 5 e7+ ♚e8 6 ♚e6 stalemate. **2...♚f8 3 e7+ ♚e8 4 ♚e6 stalemate.**

If it is Black to move then after **I...♚f7 2 e6+ ♚e7 3 ♚e5** once again **3...♚e8** is the answer so he can face the opponent's king after either **4 ♚d6** or **4 ♚f6**

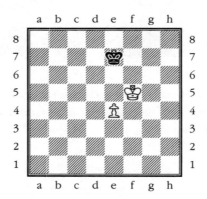

White to move wins – Black to move draws

White to move:

I ♚e5! Knowing that the previous example is a draw, White can change his strategy. Now Black will have to give way in the face-off. **I...♚d7** Or 1...♚e8 2 ♚e6 ♚f8 3 ♚d7! ♚f7 4 e5 and the pawn marches on as White controls the queening square. **2 ♚f6 ♚e8** Or 2...♚d6 3 e5+ ♚d7 4 ♚f7 and the pawn again promotes. **3 ♚e6** 3 e5 also wins in view of 3...♚f8 4 e6 ♚e8 5 e7 ♚d7 6 ♚f7. **3...♚d8 4 ♚f7** The king is now ideally placed to shepherd home the e-pawn. **4...♔d7 5 e5 ♔d8 6 e6 ♔c7 7 e7** and the pawn becomes a queen.

Black to move:

1...♔f7 2 ♔e5 Or 2 e5 transposing to the drawn endgame in the last but one diagram. **2...♔e7** The key move. Now it is *White* to move which, compared to the previous example, makes all the difference – because Black is in a position to face-off the enemy king whenever it advances. **3 ♔d5** If 3 ♔f5 Black replies 3...♔f7 and because White cannot force the king to give way he must advance his pawn and allow a stalemate: **3...♔d7 4 e5 ♔e7 5 e6 ♔e8 6 ♔d6 ♔d8 7 e7+ ♔e8 8 ♔e6 stalemate.**

More pawns

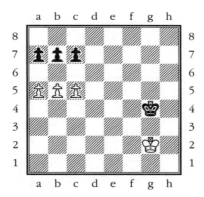

White to move and win

An important device in pawn endgames is to create a passed pawn by using other pawns as a decoy. In the above diagram it seems the black king will triumph by moving across to the queenside and capturing the white pawns. But in fact it is White who can win – with a standard trick:

1 b6! To deflect Black's a7 or c7 pawn from its respective file. **1...cxb6** After 1...axb6 there is a parallel finish to our main line with 2 c6!. **2 a6!** Clearing a path for the white pawn to march on to the eighth rank. **2...bxa6 3 c6** and the pawn promotes to a queen.

On the other hand if it were Black to move then he would win with **1...♔f5** intending to go over to the queenside and gobble up the white pawns. Then **2 b6** fails because the defending king is close enough to stop any pawn promotion. Thus: **2...cxb6** But not 2...axb6? 3 c6 bxc6 4 a6 and the distant passed pawn queens. **3 a6 bxa6 4 c6 ♔e6** and the black king catches the c-pawn just in time.

Rook endgames

Rook endgames are far more common than those with other pieces. I have selected five building blocks which should help you to handle the basics of this type of endgame.

The top five

1

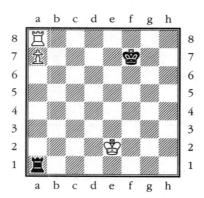

White to move wins – Black to move draws

The *White to move win* is by **1 ♖h8!** threatening to promote the pawn and if Black captures **1...♖xa7** then comes the devastating **2 ♖h7+** followed by 3 ♖xa7 winning the rook and the game.

The *Black to move draw* is by **1...♔g7** to stop the above trick and to continue shuffling the king from h7 to g7 until a critical moment arises. Of course moves such as **1...♔f6** allow **2 ♖f8+** followed by a pawn promotion.

Play might then continue **2 ♔d3 ♔h7 3 ♔c4 ♔g7 4 ♔c5 ♔h7 5 ♔b6** Protecting the pawn – now the rook on a8 can vacate the queening square. It is at this moment that Black must start checking and so force the white king to retreat: **5...♖b1+ 6 ♔a5 ♖a1+ 7 ♔b4 ♖b1+ 8 ♔a3 ♖a1+ 9 ♔b2 ♖a6 10 ♔b3 ♖a1 11 ♔b4** and we will soon be back where we started.

2

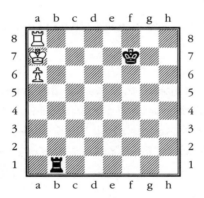

White to move wins

This is a little different because the white king has been allowed to support the a-pawn and hide from the checks by using the pawn as a shield. This is because the a-pawn is on a6 and not a7. **1 ♖b8 ♖a1 2 ♔b7 ♖b1+ 3 ♔a8!** Still hiding from the checks but allowing the a-pawn to advance. **3...♖a1 4 a7 ♔e7 5 ♔b7 ♖b1+ 6 ♔c6** and Black will eventually run out of checks – giving White a tempo to promote the pawn.

3

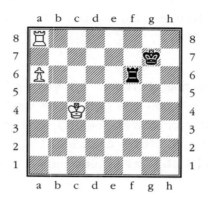

Black to move draws

Here is an effective device which can help you draw a game that might seem lost.

If White is ever tempted to advance the a-pawn then ...♖a6 will transpose to the first diagram and a draw would be the result. Therefore, with either player to move, the result is a draw. Having a defending rook on the sixth rank makes it impossible for White's king to hide from the checks by getting behind the a-pawn. For example: **1...♖f4+ 2 ♔b5 ♖f5+ 3 ♔b6** If 3 ♔d5 ♖f5+ 4 ♔e6 ♖f6+ 5 ♔e5 ♖b6 – there are no more checks so Black waits – 6 ♔d5 ♖f6! 7 ♖a7+ ♔g6 8 ♖a8 ♔g7 and White cannot make progress. **3...♖f6+ 4 ♔a7 ♖f7+** The key idea – the a-pawn provides no cover along the *rank*. **5 ♔b8 ♖f8+ 6 ♔b7 ♖f7+ 7 ♔b6 ♖f6+ 8 ♔b5 ♖f5+ 9 ♔c4 ♖f4+** when a draw will be agreed.

4

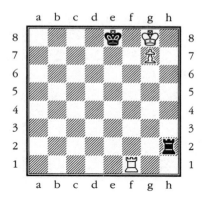

White to move wins

This is the Lucena position – named after Luis Ramirez Lucena who published it in 1497. Yes, it has been known for over 500 years!

1 ♖f4

White intends to *build a bridge* – a phrase conjured up by the great player and chess teacher Aron Nimzowitsch in the 1920s. White's basic idea is to give a check to drive the black king one file away so that his own king can move up the board and be shielded by his rook.

After the obvious 1 ♖e1+ ♔d7 2 ♔f7 Black can just keep checking. For instance 1...♖f2+ 3 ♔g6 ♖g2+ 4 ♔h7 ♖h2+ 5 ♔g8 ♖h3 6 ♖f1 ♔e7 and White has made no progress. **1...♖h1** If 1...♖e2? then 2 ♖h4 would control the h-file and introduce the simple threat of ♔h8 followed by promoting the pawn. Or 1...♔e7 2 ♖e4+ ♔d6 (2...♔f6 is met by 3 ♔f8) 3 ♔f7 ♖f2+ 4 ♔e8 ♖g2 5 ♖e7 ♖g1 6 ♖f7 intending ♔f8 to help advance the pawn. **2 ♖e4+ ♔d7 3 ♔f7 ♖f1+ 4 ♔g6 ♖g1+ 5 ♔h6 ♖h1+** If 5...♖g2 then 6 ♖e5 intending ♖g5 seals Black's fate as 6...♖h2+ 7 ♔g6 ♖g2+ 8 ♖g5 wins. **6 ♔g5 ♖g1+ 7 ♖g4 wins.**

5

Philidor 1777

Black to move

The Frenchman François-André Philidor was considered the best chess player of his time and in 1749 wrote a celebrated book entitled *L'analyse des Echecs* where he revealed his methods of play, including the above where his way of securing a draw has not been improved:

1...♖a6! Preventing the king from coming to the sixth rank is the easiest way to secure a draw. **2 ♖g7 ♖b6 3 ♖h7** If 3 ♖g6 to contest the rank then Black can enter a drawn king and pawn endgame by 3...♖xg6 4 ♔xg6 ♔e7 5 ♔f5 ♔f7 6 e6+ ♔e7 7 ♔e5 ♔e8 8 ♔f6 ♔f8 9 e7+ ♔e8 10 ♔e6 stalemate. **3...♖a6 4 e6 ♖a1!** This is the key because as soon as the pawn is advanced to the sixth rank, the rook zooms down the board ready to start checking. **5 ♔f6 ♖f1+ 6 ♔e5 ♖e1+ 7 ♔d6 ♖d1+ 8 ♔c5 ♖e1** and White cannot make progress.

General rules

1 The passed pawn should be supported by the king.

2   The defending king should be kept away from the passed pawn. This can be done by cutting it off with the rook on the rank or file.

3   If you are attacking or defending then the rook is best placed behind the passed pawn.

It is possible to use these five important rook positions to gain an understanding of a large number of more complicated rook endgames – and without having to calculate many moves over the board.

A winner

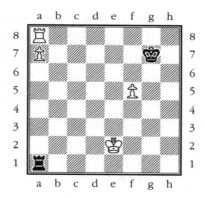

Using his endgame knowledge White will avoid wasting time marching his king up the board to b6 – only to have it continually checked. Instead he will play **1 f6+! ♚xf6** 1...♚f7 is similar to the first diagram and allows White to win with 2 ♖h8! ♖xa7 3 ♖h7+ or 1...♚h7 2 f7 and the pawn will promote. **2 ♖f8+ ♚g7 3 a8=♕** and wins.

How to defend two pawns down

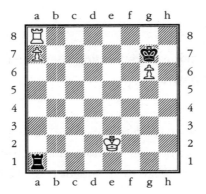

Knowing how to cope with the pawn on a7 allows Black to comfortably see ten or more moves ahead. He will know from the previous diagram that when the white king draws close to the a-pawn, the rook can continually check it and no progress can be made. Here White cannot exploit his two-pawn advantage as Black just keeps moving his rook up and down the a-file. This would also apply if White had a pawn on h6 instead of one on g6. So you could save this endgame position with Black – and perhaps avoid it at an earlier stage as White.

How to win

A celebrated endgame has provided me with inspiration and I often use it as a coaching tool because the theme can occur in so many rook and pawn endgames.

It was played in the world championship match between Alekhine and Capablanca in 1927 at a time when Capa was not only considered virtually unbeatable but also a virtuoso in the endgame – which makes Alekhine's achievement all the more meritorious.

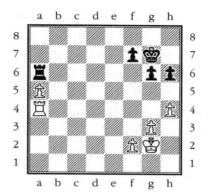

Alekhine – Capablanca

Game 34, World Championship match, Buenos Aires 1927

White has followed general principles by placing his rook behind the pawn and now needs to move his king over to the queenside to support the a-pawn. But while White is doing this the black king might proceed to mop up the kingside pawns.

54...♔f6 55 ♔f3 ♔e5 56 ♔e3 h5 57 ♔d3 ♔d5 58 ♔c3 ♔c5 Black stops the white king from advancing via the b4 and b5 squares. **59 ♖a2!** White waits to see what Black will do – so he retreats, which is one of the advantages of having the rook behind the pawn because you can adopt a wait and see policy without damaging your position. **59...♔b5** Instead 59...♔d5? would only accelerate his defeat: 60 ♔b4 ♔c6 61 ♔c4 and White can just move his rook up and down the file while Black has no good waiting moves. This will allow White to advance the a-pawn and deflect the black king away from the kingside pawns. **60 ♔b3 ♔c5 61 ♔c3 ♔b5**

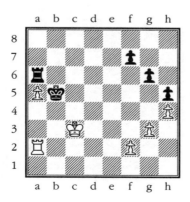

62 ♔d4! White is back on track. He aims to transfer the king to the trio of pawns on the kingside while Black is dealing with the a-pawn. **62...♖d6+** Or 62...♔b4 63 ♖a1! ♔b3 64 ♔c5 and the white king will assist with the advance of the a-pawn. **63 ♔e5 ♖e6+ 64 ♔f4 ♔a6** Now the role of blockader has passed from rook to king. Instead 64...f6 would allow a winning king and pawn endgame after 65 a6! ♖xa6 66 ♖xa6 ♔xa6 67 ♔e4. **65 ♔g5 ♖e5+ 66 ♔h6 ♖f5**

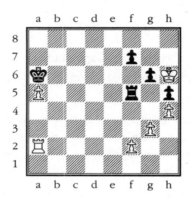

67 f4?! Even the best players in the world can make a mistake – 67 ♔g7 would have won quickly: 67...♖f3 68 ♔g8! (a waiting move) 68...♖f6 (68...f5 69 ♔g7 f4 70 ♔xg6 fxg3 71 fxg3 ♖axg3+ 72 ♔xh5 wins) 69 f4 ♖f5 70 ♔g7 is decisive because Black runs out of useful moves. If the rook moves – the f-pawn falls. If the king moves – the a-pawn advances. **67...♖c5! 68 ♖a3 ♖c7 69 ♔g7 ♖d7**

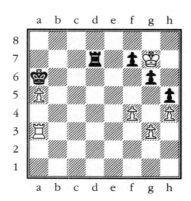

70 f5?! Imprecise. He should play 70 ♔f6! when 70...♖c7 71 f5 gxf5 (or 71...♖c6+ 72 ♔xf7 gxf5 73 ♖f3 wins) 72 ♔xf5 ♖c5+ 73 ♔f6 ♖c7 74 ♔g8 intending ♖a3-f3 and Black's kingside is busted. **70...gxf5 71 ♔h6 f4** Or 71...♔b7 72 ♖e5 ♖xf4 73 ♔g5 ♖f1 74 ♖f5! winning. **72 gxf4 ♖d5 73 ♔g7 ♖f5** If 73...♖d7 White has 74 f5 ♖c7 75 f6 with a view to ♖a3-e7 winning. **74 ♖a4 ♔b5 75 ♖e4 ♔a6 76 ♔h6! ♖xa5 77 ♖e5 ♖a1 78 ♔xh5 ♖g1 79 ♖g5 ♖h1 80 ♖f5 ♔b6 81 ♖xf7 ♔c6 82 ♖e7 1-0**

This is quite a lengthy endgame but it demonstrates how to win with an outside passed pawn – invaluable knowledge for practical play. It is also well worth remembering since this sort of situation occurs frequently. Black's king is lured away to deal with the enemy passed pawn – whereupon the white king invades and destroys the kingside.

Rook versus passed pawns

It is wrong to think that endgames are all work and no play. Even apparently simple positions can have their beauty.

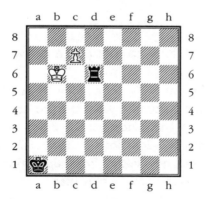

Saavedra 1895

I first saw this position when I was a junior at the local chess club and the question was "White to move, what result?" I thought it was an obvious draw but was surprised to find that the position had hidden possibilities: **1 ♔b5** Both 1 ♔b7? and 1 ♔a7? allow 1...♖d7 pinning and winning the dangerous passed pawn on the next move – and securing the draw. Of course I ♔a5?? is met by I...♖c6 and Black even wins. **I...♖d5+ 2 ♔b4** 2 ♔b6 ♖d6+ would merely repeat the position. And if the king goes to the c-file, the rook retreats and prepares to check: 2 ♔c6 ♖dI 3 c8=♕ ♖cI+ 4 ♔b7 ♖xc8 5 ♔xc8 draw. **2...♖d4+ 3 ♔b3 ♖d3+ 4 ♔c2 ♖d4!** **5 c8=♖!!** The remarkable discovery of Fernando Saavedra, a Spanish monk who was residing in Scotland at the time. He managed to achieve chess fame by improving on the solution to an endgame study that originally appeared in the *Glasgow Weekly Citizen*: 5 c8=♕ ♖c4+ 6 ♕xc4 stalemate. But after the promotion to a *rook* this line does not work. **5...♖a4** Otherwise White will mate on the h-file, **6 ♔b3** with the decisive threat of ♔xa4 and ♖cI checkmate.

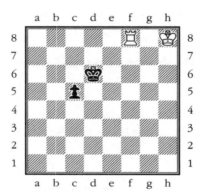

Black to move can draw

This is the sort of position that frequently arises when the black king is helping to advance the c-pawn towards the promotion square and White has to sacrifice his rook and concede a draw. But it is not quite as easy as it looks. After **I...c4??** Black is lost in view of **2 ♖f5!** This is decisive because the black king is now cut off from supporting the pawn. Naturally 2 ♖c8 was the expected move when Black will eventually draw after 2...♔d5. **2...c3 3 ♖f3 c2 4 ♖c3** and White wins the pawn and the game.

The way to draw is **I...♔d5!**, keeping close to the pawn, when a sample line runs **2 ♖d8+ ♔e4 3 ♔g7 c4 4 ♔f6 c3 5 ♖c8 ♔d3 6 ♔e5 c2 7 ♖d8+ ♔e2 8 ♖c8 ♔d1 9 ♖d8+ ♔e2 10 ♖c8 ♔d1** and White cannot make progress.

The reason why a pair of connected passed pawns is held in such high esteem is that they are difficult to stop even when you have an extra rook:

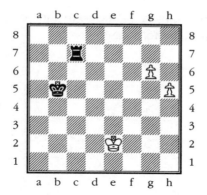

1 h6 Once both pawns are on the sixth rank a rook cannot stop the advance of at least one of them unless there is some other decisive factor in the position – such as a threat of mate. **1...♖c6 2 g7 ♖g6 3 h7 ♖xg7 4 h8=♕** with a winning position.

Now for an example from practical play:

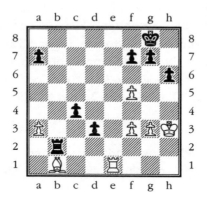

Lautier – Karpov
Linares 1995

Black played **42...♖xb1!** and White resigned. A world champion like Karpov would have instantly decided on this sacrifice because he knows instinctively that two pawns on the sixth rank beat a rook. Therefore this sort of move that normally appears in puzzle books is not as difficult to find as might first appear. Another example of how the application of a few endgame techniques in practical play can help to win more games.

The creation of two pawns on the sixth can come about in surprising circumstances, such as the following:

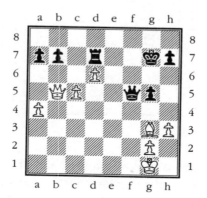

Carlsen – Navara
Wijk aan Zee 2007

Even a world class player like Magnus Carlsen can forget about the power of two pawns on the sixth rank. Here he continued 32 a5 and after 32...a6 it was Black who went on to win. Instead **32 c6!** was immediately decisive because the discovered attack on the enemy queen forces exchanges to a winning endgame **32...♕xb5** or 32...♖f7 33 ♕xf5 ♖xf5 34 c7 ♖c5 35 d7 wins **33 axb5 bxc6 34 bxc6 ♖d8 35 c7 ♖c8 36 d7** and Black can resign.

Also bear in mind rook endgames often contain checkmating opportunities. Here are couple of examples to show that anything is possible:

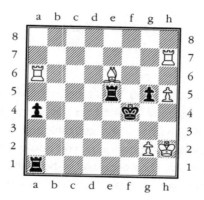

Donner – Spanjaard
Leeuwarden 1961

Black appears to be suffering but he spots a clever mating idea: **1...♖h1+! 2 ♔xh1 ♔g3 0-1** White resigned as he cannot avoid a back rank mate.

Indeed this particular back rank mate is well worth remembering because it is a recurring theme. In the next diagram the chess world was surprised when a former women's world champion was beaten by a computer. The experts said the finish was a brilliant machine move but it was in fact merely a variation on our theme:

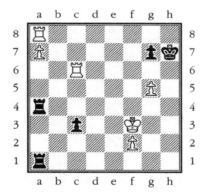

P.ConNers – Chiburdanidze
Bad Worishofen 2002

1 ♖h8+! The star move but one with which we should now be familiar. **1...♔xh8 2 g6** and Black resigned before she was mated by **♖c8** mate.

The queen

Some rook endgames end up as queen versus rook which is theoretically winning. This is all very well but there is still a lot of work to do – and remember you only have 50 moves to checkmate otherwise the game is declared a draw.

General rules

1 Activate your king and force the opponent's to the edge of the board.

2 Force the opponent's king into the corner.

3 Use your king and queen in the corner to force the rook to move away from the protection of the king.

4 Aim for the Philidor position known to be winning since 1777.

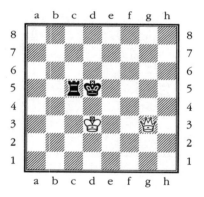

The analysis on how to win from this position is based on the classic work of Paul Keres. The Estonian was a world class player but his name also sometimes crops up in quiz shows – because he is the only chess player whose image appears on a banknote in his native country. Anyway play proceeds... **1 ♕f3+ ♚e5 2 ♕e4+ ♚d6 3 ♚d4 ♖c6** Rather than retreat immediately Black moves his rook along the rank for a few more moves in an effort to frustrate White's intentions. If 3...♖a5 4 ♕g6+ ♚d7 5 ♕f6 ♖b5 6 ♕f7+ ♚d6 7 ♕f8+ ♚d7 8 ♕f6 (The point of this little dance by the queen is to ensure that it is Black to move in this position) 8...♖a5 9 ♚c4 ♚c7 10 ♕e7+ ♚c6 11 ♕e6+ ♚c7 12 ♚b4 and the rook is forced back because 12...♖g5 (12...♖h5 13 ♕f7+ wins) 13 ♕e7+ wins. **4 ♕e5+**

♔d7 5 ♔d5 White is following the rule of forcing the opponent's king to the edge of the board. 5...♖c7 In this particular position the sixth rank defence – which is analysed later – does not quite work: 5...♖a6 6 ♕g7+ ♔d8 7 ♕f8+ ♔d7 8 ♕f7+ ♔d8 9 ♔c5 because 9...♔c8 is well met by 10 ♕e7. 6 ♕e6+ ♔d8 7 ♕g8+ 7 ♔d6? looks convincing but 7...♖c6+! forces a draw. 7...♔d7 8 ♕g7+ ♔d8 9 ♕f8+ ♔d7 10 ♕f4 ♔c8 Or 10...♖b7 11 ♕f7+ ♔c8 12 ♕e8+ ♔c7 13 ♔c5 (The general rule of forcing the black king into the corner makes it easier to form the right plan) 13...♖a7 14 ♕e7+ ♔b8 15 ♕d8+ ♔b7 16 ♔b5 ♖a8 17 ♕d7+ ♔b8 18 ♔b6 with mate to follow. 11 ♔d6 ♔b8 12 ♕e5! ♖b7 13 ♔c6+ ♔a8 14 ♕a1+ This looks odd but when you reach Philidor's position it needs to be *Black's* move. 14...♔b8 It goes without saying that 14...♖a7 would save a lot of time for both players because of 15 ♕h8 mate! 15 ♕a5

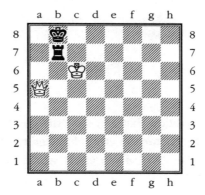

Analysis by Philidor

This is important to know because Philidor pointed out as long ago as 1777 that White could force victory from this position. Armed with such knowledge it is possible for the side with the queen to head for the critical position. 15...♖b1 The rook can run but it cannot hide. For instance: 15...♖h7 16 ♕e5+ ♔a8 17 ♕a1+ ♔b8 18 ♕b1+ and 15...♖b3 16 ♕d8+ ♔a7 17 ♕d4+ ♔b8 18 ♕f4+ ♔a7 19 ♕a4+ both win. 16 ♕d8+ ♔a7 17 ♕d4+ ♔b8 18 ♕h8+ ♔a7 19 ♕h7+ winning.

The great escape

Draw!

There is a certain position that can save the day for the defender. But before you give the computer the credit I hasten to add that it was in fact first brought to the attention of the chess world in 1782 by Domenico Lorenzo, an Italian Priest.

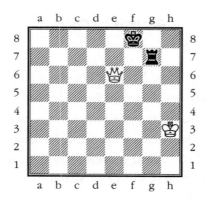

The point is that White sometimes just strolls the king up the board without thinking. But the difference here is that the close proximity of White's queen to the king leaves Black's king with few moves and allows him to draw by tactical means: **1...♖h7+ 2 ♔g4 ♖g7+ 3 ♔h5** Or 3 ♔f5 ♖f7+ 4 ♔e5 ♖e7 pinning the queen – a key feature which prevents the white king escaping the checks. Moreover 4 ♔g6 ♖g7+ 6 ♔h6 ♖h7+! 7 ♔xh7 is stalemate. **3...♖h7+ 4 ♔g6 ♖h6+! ½-½** The stalemate appears for a second time.

So it is worth carrying on in such endings just in case the winning side goes astray. The next example demonstrates what can happen after a long battle:

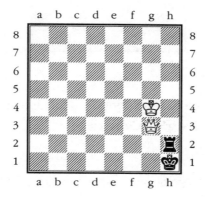

Morozevich – Jakovenko
Pamplona 2006

111 ♔f3?? It looks like White is on the verge of victory but in reality he has just blundered. He can easily win by moving the queen away to allow the black king some breathing space, for example by 111 ♕e5. **111...♖f2+!** Once again the way to force a draw is by a stalemate. **112 ♔e3 ♖e2+ 113 ♔d3 ♖d2+ 114 ♔xd2 ½-½**

Bishop endgames

The bishop can use its long range to stay out of reach of an opposing king. However in certain positions a passed pawn on the a or h-file cannot be promoted unless the queening square is of the same colour as the diagonal of the bishop. Otherwise the opposing king may be able to blockade it. For example:

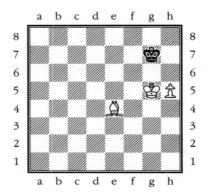

1 h6+ ♔g8 2 ♗d5+ ♔h8 Not 2...♔f8?? when 3 ♔g6 allows the h-pawn to promote. **3 ♔g6 stalemate.**

This is useful knowledge because when you are calculating far ahead and visualising such a position – you will just *know* that it's a draw.

Opposite coloured bishops

These endgames have very great drawing tendencies. Even if one of the sides is a couple of pawns ahead, the defending king and bishop can usually prevent their advance.

The next position was shown by Averbakh to be drawn:

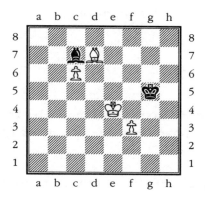

1 ♔d5 ♚f6

The priority for Black is to use his bishop to restrain the advance of White's pawns – while he will use his king to stop anything naughty from his opposite number. **2 ♔c5 ♚e7 3 ♔b5 ♚d8 4 ♔a6 ♗f4 5 ♔b7 ♗c7** and Black can hold the draw.

In an opposite coloured bishop endgame the defending side can even be *three* pawns down and still save the game.

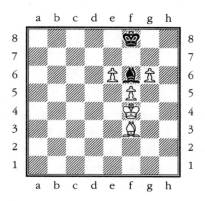

White cannot find a way to safely advance his pawns. If his king wanders over to d5 – then ...♚e7 will stop any infiltration. And if he tries to enter via h5 – then ...♚g7 also stops the white king from invading. As the white bishop is on the wrong colour diagonal it cannot oust the black king from its blockade of the dark squares.

Exceptions

General rules

1 The player with the extra pawn should try to create active play on both sides of the board in order to distract the defending king.

2 The attacking player should use his active king to assist the advance of his extra pawn.

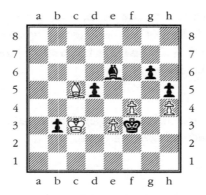

Kotov – Botvinnik
Moscow 1955

59...g5!! A clever way of creating a second passed pawn. On the other hand an immediate 59...♔g4 could be met by 60 ♗e7 protecting the h4-pawn with a likely draw. But now, if 60 hxg5, this defence is no longer available because the g5 pawn is in the way. **60 fxg5** After 60 hxg5 h4 61 ♗d6 (if 61 f5 to make room for the bishop to defend then 61...♗xf5 62 ♗d6 ♔xe3 wins because Black cannot stop *three* passed pawns) 61...♗f5 62 g6 ♗xg6 63 f5 ♗xf5 64 ♔xb3 ♔xe3 Black can use his king to shepherd the h-pawn to the queening square – which will force White to give up his bishop. **60...d4+!** So as to preserve his important b3-pawn which ties down the white king. This will enable his own king to mop up the kingside pawns without interference. **61 exd4 ♔g3 62 ♗a3 ♔xh4 63 ♔d3 ♔xg5 64 ♔e4 h4 65 ♔f3 ♗d5+ 0-1**

White resigned because if he stops the h-pawn from getting through – then the b-pawn, assisted by the white king, will cost him his bishop.

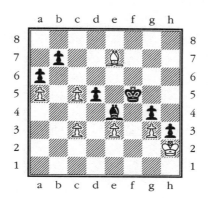

Thesing – Lane
Dutch Team Championship 2000

Though material is nominally level, White's doubled and isolated pawns are weak and his king is stuck in the corner, preventing any promotion of the passed h-pawn. White may have thought that by putting all his pawns on dark squares, they could be defended by his bishop. But this plan backfires because the pawns actually get in the way of his bishop and the light squares are terribly weak.

50...♗f3 I need to open a path for my king in order to infiltrate on the light squares and attack the weak pawns. The defensive resources of the white bishop will then be stretched to the limit. **51 c6** Sacrificing a pawn to activate his bishop. As we have already seen, being a pawn or two down in an opposite coloured bishop endgame does not necessarily mean defeat. After 51 ♗f8 ♚e4 52 ♗h6 ♚d3 Black also yields a pawn but without improving his bishop. **51...bxc6 52 ♗c5 ♚e4 53 ♗d4 ♚d3 54 ♚g1** It seems that Black is hoping to draw by sitting tight and shuffling his pieces back and forth. But Black has a concrete objective – to create a passed pawn that is a long way from the defending king. I was influenced in my thinking by the Kotov-Botvinnik position and started looking for a good way to invest my extra pawn. **54...♚c4 55 ♗e5 ♚b5 56 ♗c7 c5 57 ♗b6 c4** A committal move. It appears that White can safeguard the c and d-pawns with ♗b6-♗d4 but I had already seen the forthcoming combination designed to create a new passed pawn. **58 ♔h2**

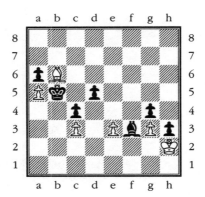

58...d4! With Botvinnik's play in mind, I found a way to reduce the influence of the defending bishop – which is overloaded with responsibilities. When I play my king to b3 I want to ensure that Black cannot defend the c3 pawn by ♗d4. **59 exd4** Now White's bishop is denied the use of the important d4 square – but he had little choice: 59 ♗xd4 allows 59...♔xa5 when the black king will assist the advance of the a-pawn, while 59 cxd4 is followed by 59...c3 and the pawn will promote to a queen. **59...♗d5 60 ♗c7 ♔a4** It now becomes clear that White needs his bishop to be on b4 to defend the c3 pawn but he cannot achieve this without losing the a5 pawn. **61 ♗d6 ♔xa5 62 ♗c7+ ♔b5 63 ♗d6 a5 64 ♗c7 a4 65 ♗d6 ♔c6** At this point I could see at least a dozen moves ahead – but that is no big deal when White can only move his bishop. I now intend the king manoeuvre ♔d7-e6-f5-e4-d3-c2-b3 to assist the a-pawn's advance – and there is nothing White can do to stop this plan. **66 ♗a3 ♔d7 0-1**

Knight endgames

Knight endgames should be treated like king and pawn endgames. The knight is a short range piece like the king and it can take some time to reach its destination – which might be critical when there is an enemy passed pawn on the loose.

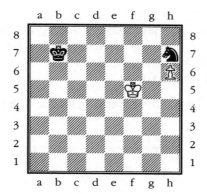

Indeed knight versus passed pawn is a quite frequent endgame scenario so it pays to know the drawing routine by heart – rather than trying to calculate it over the board.

1 ♔g6 ♘f8+ 2 ♔f7 ♘h7 3 ♔g7 ♘g5 4 ♔g6 ♘e6! This is the important move to remember – the knight moves further away from the pawn but foresees a saving fork. **5 h7 ♘f8+** and Black eliminates the dangerous pawn.

It is asking too much of a knight to defend against simultaneous advances of passed pawns on both flanks – as the limitations of its short range movements then become very apparent.

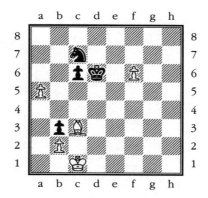

Lane – Rujevic
Fiji Zonal 2002

60 &e5+! Dragging the black king one square further away from the promotion square on f8 – and thereby leaving the knight the impossible task of coping on its own with two passed pawns on different flanks. **60...&xe5 61 f7 ♘e6** The knight can stop one pawn... **62 a6** ...but not the other. **62...&f6 63 a7 1-0**

Naturally, this changes if the defending king is well placed:

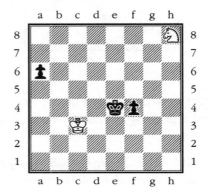

Lane – Illescas Cordoba
Chess Olympiad, Bled 2002

In this position White's king has the a-pawn under surveillance which allows his knight to concentrate on sacrificing itself for the f-pawn. **64 ♘f7 a5 65 ♘g5+** The knight is well placed to capture the f-pawn – thereby allowing the white king to stroll over and take the a-pawn. **65...&d5 66 &b3 &e5 ½-½**

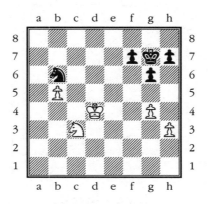

Chigorin – Marshall
Carlsbad 1907

How difficult is can be for a knight to handle a passed pawn is seen here.

70 ♘d5! White is happy to exchange pieces to allow the b-pawn to rush to promotion... **70...♘d7** ...while Black is prepared to exchange his knight for the opponent's passed b-pawn – but not for his knight. **71 g5** Preventing the black king from fast tracking into the game via f6 in an effort to eliminate all the kingside pawns. **71...h6 72 ♘f6 ♘b6 73 h4** Maintaining the pawn wedge keeps Black's king in jail. **73...hxg5 74 hxg5 ♚f8 75 ♚c5 ♘a4+ 76 ♚d6!** Chigorin prevents the release of the black king. **76...♚g7** Instead 76...♘b6? allows 77 ♘d7+ ♘xd7 78 ♚xd7 and the b-pawn will promote. **77 ♚c6 ♚f8 78 b6 ♘xb6 79 ♚xb6** White is clearly winning but it is worth seeing how this advantage is quickly put to good use. **79...♚e7 80 ♚c7 ♚f8 81 ♚d7 ♚g7 82 ♚e7 ♚h8 83 ♘e8** Not 83 ♚xf7?? – when it is suddenly a draw! **83...♚g8 84 ♚f6 1-0**

General rules

1 If the pawns are on one side of the board, the knight's short range is not so much of a problem.

2 Knights operate well in closed or blocked positions.

3 Knights do badly when trying to defend simultaneously against passed pawns on both sides of the board.

Predict-a-move

The endgame is far from being boring – in fact this phase offers plenty of opportunities for tactical possibilities. The practical player should always remain alert to the opportunity of winning material or even delivering checkmate. And even if you have your back to the wall, don't give up – there is always a chance of stalemate.

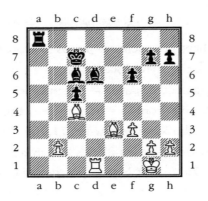

Nakamura – Muhammad
San Diego 2004

Here the position seems to be heading for a draw. However former US champion Hikaru Nakamura is a big fan of playing quick games on the Internet where tactics reign supreme – and he has used his experience to lure his opponent into a trap by playing 27 ♗c1-e3. This tempted his opponent to attack the now unprotected b2 pawn by playing **27...♖b8??** which allowed **28 ♖xd6! 1-0** Black saw too late that 28...♔xd6 29 ♗f4+ ♔d7 30 ♗xb8 leaves White with an extra piece.

Keeping the opponent's rook off the seventh rank is generally a good policy – but be careful not to overdo it...

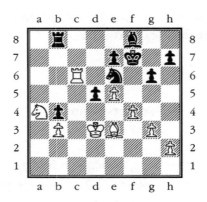

Kramnik – Shirov
Wijk aan Zee 2007

Black is already covering the c7 square with his knight but to be doubly sure he played **34...♖b7?** only to be rocked by **35 ♖xe6** After realising what he had done and not being able to face the prospect of 35...♔xe6 36 ♘c5+ forking the king and rook and leaving White a piece up – he decided to resign. **1-0**

The method can also be used to conjure up a mating attack:

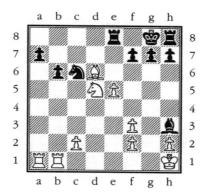

Hamdouchi – Mirzoev
Illes Medes 2007

White has moved his king into the corner in order to play ♖g1 and then ♘f6 mate as the g-pawn is pinned. Black sees what is coming and prepares to move his king out of harm's way.

21...h6 Black makes room for the king to move to h7 in order to avoid the tactical threats on the g-file. He could have tried 21...h5 to counter White's attacking ambitions but perhaps that looked rather too weakening. On the other hand after 21...♘xe5? can follow 22 ♘c7 attacking the rook which cannot move without leaving the knight undefended. **22 ♖g1 ♔h7** 22...g5 would allow 23 ♘f6+ winning material. **23 ♖xg7+!!** and **Black resigned** because of 23...♔xg7 24 ♖g1+ ♔h7 25 ♘f6 mate. The *predict-a-move* system worked because White foresaw his opponent's most obvious replies and had prepared a crushing rook sacrifice against them.

In the next position from the game **Speelman-Velimirovic,** Maribor 1980, White had to keep a close watch on Black's queenside pawn majority where a passed pawn could be created at any moment. However he had seen a neat trick to cope with that eventuality and calculated the consequences of an impressive looking sacrifice. After 23 ♗xg7 ♘xg7 White escapes with a draw by repetition after 24 ♘h6+ ♔h8 25 ♘xf7+ ♔g8 26 ♘h6+. So far, so good, but then Speelman noticed the annoying 23...♗xg7 24 ♘e7+ ♔f8 25 ♘xc8 ♗xb2 when Black is attacking another pawn on a3 and has ample compensation for the sacrificed material – especially as 26 ♖d5? fails to 26...c3 when White is in trouble. Therefore, White used the *predict-a-move* idea as a way of ridding himself of his potentially weak a3 pawn.

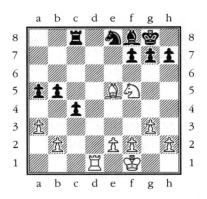

23 ♗c3! The bishop attack on the a-pawn prompted an obvious response. **23...b4** According to Speelman this was played after just three minutes thought – because it is such a natural move. However it fits neatly into White's plan... **24 axb4 axb4 25 ♗xg7 ½-½** A draw was agreed because Black would have taken with the knight and allowed a repetition of position after 25...♘xg7 26 ♘h6+ ♔h8 27 ♘xf7+ ♔g8 28 ♘h6+. Now that the a-pawns have been exchanged we see the difference: on the alternative recapture 25...♗xg7 26 ♘e7+ ♔f8 27 ♘xc8 ♗xb2 28 ♘b6 c3 29 ♘c4 it is White who now has the advantage.

General rules for the endgame

1 If you are a piece up swap off more pieces.

The fewer pieces on the board the more likely it is that the attacker can create a passed pawn or capture more pawns. The chance of a counterattack by the defender is also more remote.

2 If you are trying to draw – exchange off pawns.

The fewer pawns on the board the more chance there will be for the defender to sacrifice a piece for the last remaining one.

3 Do not make pawn moves without good reason – especially when you should be trying to improve the positions of your pieces.

Such pawn moves will create long-term weaknesses that cannot be easily rectified.

4 Make sure your pieces are well placed before creating a passed pawn.

A passed pawn might be surrounded and captured if it does not have sufficient back up of pieces.

5 In rook endgames – activate the rook.

Invading the opponent's second row is particularly advantageous as it can hit his pawns from the side where they most vulnerable. As a corollary try to restrict the movement of the opponent's rook.

6 Place your rook behind the passed pawn.

It will then promote the advance of the pawn to the queening square without getting in its way and also increase its own range of movement as the pawn advances.

7 The king is an ideal blockader of a pawn.

Therefore strive to create a passed pawn on the opposite flank where it is out of reach from the opponent's king.

8 Do not put pawns on the same colour squares as your bishop.

You may think it will help to defend your pawns but it has the downside of limiting the scope of the bishop. Also it dangerously weakens squares of the opposite colour to your bishop, leaving them particularly vulnerable to invasion by the opponent's king. If the pawns were on the opposite colour to your bishop these squares would have been protected.

9 Activate the king.

In the endgame the king becomes a stronger piece and is less likely to find itself in danger. So allow your king an active role.

10 Be on constant alert for combinations and mating threats.

Despite the reduced material the endgame still has plenty of opportunities to win material and create mating nets.

Day 7
The art of swindling

Chess Trivia — Former world champion José Raúl Capablanca did not lose a game for eight years between 10 February 1916 and 21 March 1924.

What is a swindle?

In chess parlance a swindle is when a player manages to trick his opponent and transform what appeared inevitable defeat into a win. It is also used in a more general sense to indicate the saving of a lost position by drawing or winning. In life the word 'swindle' tends to be linked to cheating or fraud – but in chess it is considered a respected art which demonstrates fighting spirit and resourcefulness even when all seems lost.

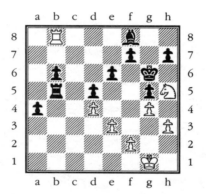

Finegold – Kuznecov
Oakham 1986

The American Ben Finegold has always impressed me by his tough defensive skills and never-give-up spirit. I suspect he was greatly encouraged as a junior when, in the following amazing game, he was able to convert a loss into an inspired victory. His Canadian opponent had played a fine game with the black pieces and was looking forward to advancing his two connected passed pawns to victory. However at this moment he showed a sudden lapse in judgement and played the over-hasty **41...a3??** It is understandable that Black can't wait to queen the pawn – but his sense of danger lets him down. Actually there is no rush and 41...♗e7! first would have forced resignation in a few moves. For example 42 ♖g8+ ♔h6 43 ♖g7 (unlike the game 43 h4 no longer works because the bishop controls the important f6 and g5 squares – so 43...gxh4 stops any mating threats) 43...a3 44 ♖xf7 ♗d8 45 ♖a7 ♖a5 winning easily. **42 ♖xf8 a2** Black had seen that 43 ♖a8 fails because of

43...♖a5 and assumed that his new queen would be enough to win. Even giving his king a flight square by 42...h6 is no help due to 43 ♖g8+ ♔h7 44 ♘f6 mate. **43 ♖g8+ ♔h6 44 h4! a1=♕+** 44...f6 45 ♘xf6 threatening 46 hxg5 mate is similar to the game. **45 ♔g2** 45 ♔h2 is an even quicker way because it avoids a pawn check. **45...gxh4**

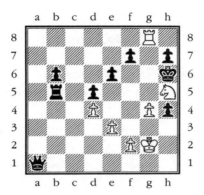

46 ♘f6! Only now does it become obvious that the threat g4-g5 mate cannot be stopped. **46...h3+ 47 ♔h2 1-0**

That was a remarkable turnaround and should encourage you never to give up. Here is another example:

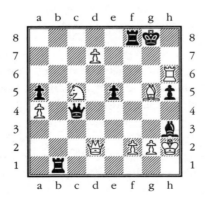

San Segundo Carrillo – Wojtaszek
Chess Olympiad, Turin 2006

Despite its apparent complexity this position is actually hopeless for Black. However, in true *predict-a-move* fashion, Black sees that his opponent will find it hard to resist promoting the pawn. Play duly continued **40 d8=♕??** The cool 40 f3 would have left him with a big advantage – but also 40 ♖g6+ ♔h7 41 ♗e7 wins because Black is mated after 41...♔xg6 42 ♕g5+. **40...♖h1+!** and White resigned in view of 41 ♔xh1 (or 41 ♔g3 ♕g4 mate) 41...♕f1+ 42 ♔h2 ♕xg2 mate. **0-1**

Houdini

The English grandmaster Tony Miles described his play in the following position with the words: "This must rank as one of my greatest Houdini impersonations."

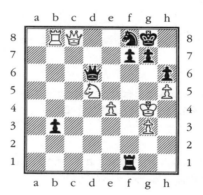

Miles – Schneider
Philadelphia 1980

It is hardly surprising that Miles likened himself to the most famous of all escapologists – Harry Houdini. Earlier he had been two pawns down and forced to march his king precariously up the board. Then Black returned one of the pawns in an effort to weave a mating net and in the diagram position he has just played 1...♖f1? – to meet 2 ♖xb3 with 2...♕e5! when 3 ♘f4 ♕xe4 maintains his advantage. However this move took the rook away from the d1 square where it was doing a good job and Miles exploited this by 1 **♕xf8+!** when the game continued: 1...**♕xf8 2 ♘e7+ ♔h7 3 ♖xf8 b2?** Black is now losing but this obvious move hastens his demise. If Black had seen White's shock reply he might have instead tried 3...♖e1 although after 4 ♔f5 ♖f1+ 5 ♔e5 ♖g1 (5...♖f6 6 ♘d5 ♖b6! 7 ♘c3 b2 8 ♘b1 is also losing for Black although he may be able to generate some swindling chances of his own) 6 ♖b8 ♖xg3 7 ♘f5 ♖h3 8 ♖b7 wins comfortably. **4 ♘g6!**

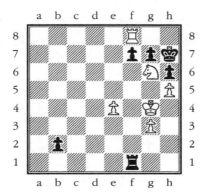

1-0 The only way to avoid checkmate by ♖h8 is 4...fxg6 which allows 5 ♖xf1 not only winning a rook but preventing the promotion of the b-pawn – to boot!

Time-trouble

It is only natural that players can go wrong when there are many moves still to make and the minutes on the chess clock are fast ticking away. If you are completely lost then this is probably the best moment to look for a swindle. And sometimes you don't need to look too hard – as in the next position which remains one of my most memorable games because of its unexpected finish:

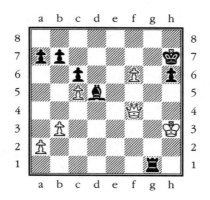

Bradbury – Lane
London 1983

I had been struggling for some time but encouraged by my opponent's desperate attempts to make the time-control I carried on – more in hope than expectation – with **57...♗e6+** At this point White leaned over and played 58 ♕c7 when I was embarrassingly forced to mutter "Check". White resigned instantly because the touch move rule obliges White to interpose his queen to block the check – thereby losing instantly. This incident came about because tournament etiquette does not require you to say "Check!" as it assumes that your opponent will notice it anyway. I have to add that Neil Bradbury took the loss with good grace – which is the right way to deal with such a situation. It is certainly not acceptable behaviour to sweep the pieces from the board since you will get a reputation for being a bad loser – as a consequence of which future opponents may try just that little bit harder to beat you.

If your opponent is struggling to make the time-limit, there is even more likelihood of pulling off a swindle. But you will need a little luck as well...

Ward – Summerscale
British Championship 1992

1 d4 d5 2 c4 c6 3 ♘c3 ♘f6 4 e3 e6 5 ♘f3 ♘bd7 6 ♕c2 7 b3 0-0 8 ♗d3 dxc4

8...b6, intending a queenside fianchetto, is probably an improvement. Then he would retain the option of exchanging on c4 at a more suitable moment.

9 bxc4 c5 10 0-0 cxd4 11 exd4 b6 12 ♘e5 ♗b7 13 ♖e1 ♖e8 14 ♖e3

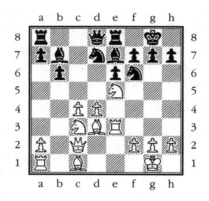

Though this looks like the caveman approach, White's rather crude attack offers good practical chances because Black must defend very precisely. Alternatively, development by 14 ♗g5 looks good since 14...♘f8 15 ♖ad1 gives White a slight initiative since 15...♕xd4? 16 ♗xh7+ would win the queen with a discovered attack.

14...♘f8 15 ♘e2 ♘6d7 16 ♖h3 ♘g6 17 ♗xg6 hxg6??

Capturing towards the centre is the general rule but each position should be judged on its own merits. And here 17...fxg6 is correct – since the weakness of the isolated e6 pawn is compensated by the active bishop on b7.

18 ♖h8+!

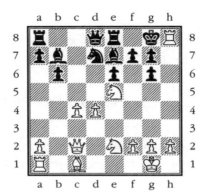

A neat combination that sets up a 'family fork' of the king and queen. At this point Black might well have resigned but in his notes to the game in *Kingpin* magazine Aaron Summerscale saw the funny side. He wrote : "I wished the ground would open up and swallow me. I had a very important choice to make: resign now and ease the pain or play on to avoid appearing in the next book of miniatures."

18...♔xh8 19 ♘xf7+ ♔h7 20 ♘xd8 ♖axd8

Black has a terrible position but if you are a fighter there is always hope. Summerscale added his own thoughts "I played this move and resolved to resign at move 40 if he made the time-control. He had a whole half hour left but it gave me a goal to play towards. Strangely though, from this moment on he began to consume large quantities of time. Maybe he still had one eye on the miniature and was looking for the most brilliant win, but from now on I defended resolutely."

The short-term goal of making the time control and the fact that he has rook and knight for the queen provides enough encouragement for Black to continue. It is even acceptable to play on if you have lost a knight or a bishop – but not more than that unless you have compensation. In the present situation there is one other factor that might come into play – his opponent could go wrong in time-trouble.

The defender should remain calm and not make any reckless sacrifices. Though White's task should be straightforward he has to choose his method of attack carefully as there are several options – some better than others.

21 ♘f4 ♘f8 22 ♗b2 ♗g5

Black waits patiently...

23 ♘h3 ♗f6 24 ♖d1 ♖d7 25 ♗a3

Tactically this is a good choice and could cause problems if it is followed up in the right way. However, with the clock ticking away, it might have been better to play it safe with 25 ♘f4 – intending to meet 25...♖ed8 with 26 ♘e2 to stop any sign of counterplay and edge closer to the time-control at move 40 when he will have more time to plot his victory.

25...♗xd4

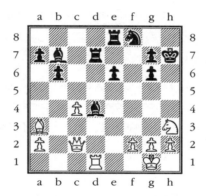

26 ♕a4

White threatens ♗xf8 followed by ♕xd7 but this is obvious and easily rebuffed. He could have pressed home the advantage with 26 ♘g5+! ♚g8 (26...♚h8 is weak due to 27 ♕a4 with the threat of ♗xf8 and ♘xe6 with similar play to the game – and 27...♖dd8 is useless because of the knight fork 28 ♘f7+) 27 ♚h1 stopping any tricks. The difference from the game is that the knight is active and makes ♗xf8 followed by ♕xg6 a dangerous threat.

26...♖dd8 27 ♕xa7 ♖d7 28 ♕a4 ♖a8 29 ♕b3 ♗c6

At last Black has a tactic. It is a pity that ...♗a4 can easily be prevented but at least he is moving in the right direction.

30 ♕g3 e5 31 ♗xf8 ♖xf8 32 ♚h1?

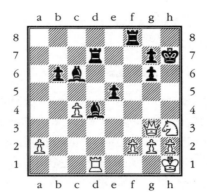

The pressure on the f2 pawn induces White to tuck his king away in the corner. A little more time would have enabled him to find 32 ♕g4! maintaining his clear advantage.

32...♗xf2!

A nice trick to get right back into the game – 33 ♘xf2 ♖xd1+ 34 ♘xd1 ♖f1 is checkmate. The bishop move would certainly frighten any time troubled player who is still reflecting: "What happened to my brilliancy prize?"

33 ♕b3 ♗e3!

Crafty play. In time pressure Summerscale prevents his opponent's planned ♖xd7 – which now fails because of ...♖f1 mate.

34 ♖e1 ♖d2

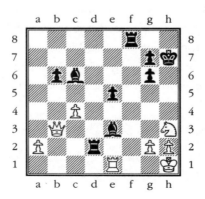

Now it is Black who is having all the fun by bringing a rook to the second rank and targeting the g2 pawn.

35 ♕xe3 ♖xg2 36 ♕e4?

The bishop looks deadly on the a8-h1 diagonal so Ward feels compelled to block it – even though giving back the queen still loses. With more time on the clock he might have found the surprising 36 ♘f4! ♖e2+ (if the knight is taken then White gets out of trouble: 36...exf4? 37 ♕h3+ ♔g8 38 ♕e6+ ♔h7 39 ♕xc6 or 36...♖xf4? 37 ♕h3+ ♔g8 38 ♕c8+ ♔h7 39 ♕xc6 wins) 37 ♘d5 ♖f1+! 38 ♖xf1 ♖xe3 – with a superior endgame but at least White is hanging on.

36...♗xe4 37 ♖xe4 ♖xa2 38 ♖xe5 ♖f1+ 39 ♘g1 ♖ff2 0-1

A perfect swindle

General rules

1   In losing positions continue to put up maximum resistance. Do not resort to reckless tactics which will leave you in a hopeless state if they fail.

2   Try to lure the opponent into time-trouble where a blunder is more likely.

3   Try to set stalemate traps in the endgame.

4   Play actively and use every opportunity to attack.

5   Remember that nobody ever won a game by resigning!

Sometimes it can be a fine line between swindling and losing. The best example I can think of is the following:

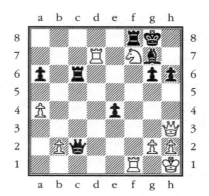

Schneider – Tal
Chess Olympiad, Lucerne 1982

Black has just played 29...♔g8 to avoid the draw by repetition after 29...♔h7 30 ♘g5+ ♔h8 31 ♘f7+ ♔h7 32 ♘g5+. But this should have backfired as White could have won with the spectacular 30 ♕xh6!! when 30...♗xh6 31 ♘xh6+ ♔h8 32 ♖xf8 is mate. But Tal's opponent missed his chance and continued **30 g3? h5 31 ♘g5 ♕xb2 32 ♘e6 ♖xf1+ 33 ♕xf1 ♗f6 34 ♖d8+ ♔f7!** Not 34...♗xd8? which allows a perpetual check after 35 ♕f8+ ♔h7 36 ♕f7+ ♔h6 37 ♕f8+ ♔h7 38 ♕f7+. **35 ♘g5+ ♔e7 36 ♘xe4 ♔xd8 0-1**

Stalemate

Even though all may seem lost you can still set traps for your opponent.

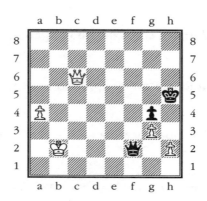

Burmakin – Ivanov
Seville 2007

In a lost position Black has started checking – to make his opponent work for the full point. And remarkably it paid off when White decided on **58 ♔c3?** rather than the obvious and good 58 ♕c2 – blocking the check and remaining a couple of pawns up. Then came the sensational **58...♕f6+!** whereupon a draw was agreed because 59 ♕xf6 is stalemate!

A commitment to carry on until all possibilities of saving the game are exhausted has to be the best practical advice:

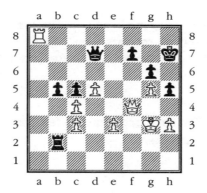

Chernin – Dunnington
Cappelle la Grande 1994

The position is quite hopeless and White could not understand why his opponent was playing on. I was watching the game and noticed his impatience. **41...bxc4** This is a clever reply because Black is refusing to give up and now finds a way to hang on to the game by a thread. **42 ♕f6??** Though this looks like the end because of the threatened checkmate on h8, a little extra thought would have found 42 ♕e5! leaving Black with a lost position. **42...h4+** A desperate check but it has hidden qualities. **43 ♔xh4** Instead 43 ♔f4 runs into 43...♖f2+ winning the queen while 43 ♔f3 ♕xd5+ 44 ♔g4 ♕d1+ (44 ...♕xa8 45 ♕xf7+ ♔h8 46 ♕f6+ leads to a draw) 45 ♔xh4 (45 ♔f4 allows 45...♖f2+) 45...♕e1+ 46 ♔g4 ♖g2+ winning. **43...♖b8!**

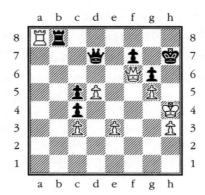

White missed this amazing move and now realised he had thrown away the win. If the white rook retreats then ...♛xd5 secures equality so he decided to allow the spectacular stalemate finish. **44 ♖xb8 ♛xh3+! 45 ♔xh3 ½-½**

So never give up. You could score quite a few more points by pulling off a swindle every now and then.

Moving on

A good way to improve is to play lots of games – especially against opponents who are slightly stronger than you. If that is not possible you can go on to the internet where you will find a ready supply of opponents from all over the world. Chess software also provides useful material for study and testing your skills – but make sure it is designed for your level of play.

More books

For improving players:

Find the Winning Move by Gary Lane published by Batsford.

A collection of puzzles to test your strength.

http://www.papertiger.co.uk/category/chess/index.jsp

For advanced players:

Think Like A Grandmaster by Alexander Kotov published by Batsford.

A guide on how to improve your thinking during a game.

Chess: The art of logical thinking by Neil McDonald published by Batsford

A selection of instructive games with explanations after every move.

Computer software

For improving players

Learn Chess with Martika

A stylish, animated girl guides you through over 400 puzzles. An interactive programme where Martika speaks and gives tips on how to improve.

http://www.learnchess.info

For advanced players

Fritz 10 produced by Chessbase.

This is the computer programme used by top players to analyse their games. It can also be used to practice and improve – and it even makes witty comments when you play bad moves!

ChessBase 9 produced by Chessbase.

A programme to store, sort and analyse games. The main database has over 3 million games.

Useful websites

Pittsburgh University chess site – Free Software available

www.pitt.edu/~schach/Archives/index2.html

News on how to play chess by post or e-mail. www.iccf.com

History of Chess

http://www.chesshistory.com

The Week in Chess – A comprehensive round up of the most recent international news, games and gossip.

www.chesscenter.com/twic/twic.html

Chess Today – A daily chess newspaper with annotated games is sent to a subscriber's e-mail address. Free sample copies are available. The service has been running since 2000 by Russian grandmaster Alex Baburin who now resides in Ireland where he is the No. I player.

3 Eagle Hill, Blackrock, Co. Dublin, Ireland.

http://www.chesstoday.net/

Chess Federations

If you want to obtain more information on chess clubs or tournaments in your area then please contact your national organisation:

The World Chess Federation

www.fide.com

The Australian Chess Federation

No permanent address but information available from national chess magazine:

Australian Chess

PO Box 370

Riverstone

NSW 2765

http://www.chessaustralia.com.au

Canadian Chess Federation

E1-2122 Gladwin Crescent,

Ottawa

Ontario K1B 5N1

http://www.chess.ca/

The English Chess Federation

The Watch Oak,

Chain Lane,

Battle,

East Sussex TN33 OYD

http://www.englishchess.org.uk/

The Irish Chess Federation

1 Templeview Lawn

Clare Hall

Dublin 13

http://www.icu.ie

The Northern Ireland Federation

http://www.ulsterchess.org/

The Scottish Chess Federation

39 Morningside Park

Edinburgh

EH10 5EZ

http://www.chessscotland.com/

The Welsh Chess Federation

http://www.welshchessunion.co.uk/

The New Zealand Chess Federation

No permanent address but information available from the national chess magazine:

New Zealand Chess Magazine

PO Box 1627

Taupo

http://www.nzchess.co.nz/

The USA Chess Federation

US Chess Federation

PO Box 3967,

Crossville, TN 38557

http://www.uschess.org

Glossary of chess terms

Blitz

Speed chess timed by a chess clock that is normally set at five minutes per player for the entire game.

Blunder

A bad mistake that usually leads to a loss of material or being checkmated. A blunder can instantly convert a winning position into a losing one.

Capture

The act of capturing a piece or pawn.

Castling

The only time in chess when you are allowed to make two moves on one turn. From its starting position a previously unmoved king goes two squares to the left or right and the rook jumps over its head and lands next to it. You cannot castle out of check, into check or over check.

Caveman

A blatant attacking player whose aim is to checkmate you – come what may.

Centre

The squares e4, d4, d5 and e5 – in the middle of the chessboard.

Check

When the king is attacked.

Checkmate

When the king is attacked and can't get out of check. Game over.

Development

The act of moving the pieces from their original squares and into play.

Endgame

The final phase of the game where few pieces remain.

En passant

A special rule which enables a pawn on the fifth rank (or fourth for Black) to capture an opposing pawn that has just moved two squares – thus treating it as if it had just moved one square.

En prise

A pawn or a piece that is exposed to attack and can be captured.

Equality

A position with equal chances.

Exchange sacrifice

When you give up a rook for a knight or bishop.

Fianchetto

When a bishop is developed in the opening on b2 or g2 (or b7 or g7 for Black) within the pawn triangle a2-b3-c2 or f2-g3-h2 (or a7-b6-c7 or f7-g6-h7 for Black). It is an Italian term and is pronounced 'fyan-ket-to'

FIDE

An acronym for the World Chess Federation which is known by its official French title: 'Fédération internationale des échecs'. It is pronounced 'fee-day'.

File

A vertical row of squares on the board.

Fork

When one piece attacks two or more pieces at the same time.

Kingside

The side of the board on which the king starts the game and consisting of the squares on the e, f, g and h files.

Gambit

When material is given away for initiative or attack. It usually refers to an opening variation e.g. King's Gambit, Scotch Gambit etc.

Manoeuvre

A sequence of moves by one piece – with an objective in view.

Mate

A shortened form of the word checkmate.

Middlegame

The phase of the game that follows the opening. It is the time when attacking or defensive plans are usually made.

Notation

The code for recording chess moves. The official notation used today is the algebraic version.

Opening

The first phase of the game where usually the pieces are developed and the kings castled.

Opening theory

Knowledge of the chess openings contained in books and computer databases.

Opponent

The person you are playing against.

Patzer

A humorous or even derogatory term for a bad chessplayer. However it is relative because there is always somebody worse than you. Other popular words for an inept chessplayer are rabbit and fish.

Perpetual check

When a player's king is caught in an unending series of checks – at this point the game is declared a draw.

Pin

A piece is attacked and if it moves a more valuable piece behind it will be taken.

Predict-a-move

Foreseeing the opponent's intended moves and laying a trap accordingly. If the opponent blindly falls into the trap he will usually suffer significant damage.

Queen's side

The side of the board where the queen starts the game and consisting of the squares on the a, b, c and d files.

Rank

A horizontal row of squares across the board.

Rating

Any chessplayer who plays in tournaments or club competitions has a rating. The international standard is the Elo rating system named after the Hungarian Arpad Elo who devised it. The world champion is rated about 2800, a grandmaster 2500, an international master 2400 and club player 1800.

Resign

To give up the game as a loss before being checkmated. This can be done by reaching out for a handshake and saying "I resign" or the more traditional method of knocking over your king.

Sacrifice

When a pawn or a piece is given up with some ulterior motive in mind.

Skewer

A piece is attacked and if it moves then one of lesser value behind it can be taken.

Simultaneous display

A strong player takes on a number of opponents – usually twenty or more – at the same time. The boards are arranged in a circle and the master moves from one board to the next – making one move at a time until he comes round again. The master usually takes the white pieces in all games.

Stalemate

When the king is not in check but has no legal move. At this point the game is abandoned as a draw.

Strategy

A plan of action to achieve a concrete objective – either in the short or long-term.

Swindle

Tricking an opponent when the chips are down – thereby converting a loss into a draw or a win.

Tactics

A forcing sequence of moves that leads to checkmate or positional/material gain.

Time-trouble

In a game played with a chess clock a player has to complete a certain number of moves within the time allocated. If you still have a number of moves to make and there is hardly any time left on the clock you are said to be in time-trouble.

Touch move

If you touch a piece when it is your turn – you have to move it.

Zugzwang

A German word meaning 'compulsion to move'. It is a player's turn to move – but all moves lead to trouble. It is of particular importance in king and pawn endgames.

Other Batsford chess titles currently available:

Advance and Other Anti-French Variations
Lev Psakhis
0 7134 8843 3
£14.99

An Attacking Repertoire for White
Sam Collins
0 7134 8910 3
£15.99

The Bishop's Opening Explained
Gary Lane
0 7134 8917 0
£14.99

Black is OK Forever!
András Adorján
0 7134 8942 1
£15.99

Black is Still OK!
András Adorján
0 7134 8870 0
£15.99

The Chess Player's Bible
James Eade
0 7134 89251
£14.99

Chess Tactics
Paul Littlewood
0 7134 8934 0
£12.99

Chess: The Art of Logical Thinking
Neil McDonald
0 7134 8894 8
£14.99

Find the Winning Move
Gary Lane
0 7134 8871 9
£14.99

French Defence: Steinitz, Classical and Other Systems
Lev Psakhis
0 7134 8941 3
£15.99

Ideas Behind Modern Chess Openings
Gary Lane
0 7134 8715 7
£14.99

Ideas Behind Modern Chess Openings: Black
Gary Lane
0 7134 8950 2
£15.99

Imagination in Chess
Paata Gaprindashvili
0 7134 8935 9
£12.99

Judit Polgar: The Princess of Chess
Tibor Karolyi
0 7134 8890 5
£15.99

Logical Chess: Move by Move
Irving Chernev
0 7134 8464 0
£14.99

Najdorf: Life and Games
Tomasz Lissowski, Adrian Mikhalchishin and Miguel Najdorf
0 7134 8920 0
£14.99

Rethinking the Chess Pieces
Andrew Soltis
0 7134 8904 9
£14.99

Test Your Chess with Daniel King
Daniel King
0 7134 8900 6
£14.99

Tony Miles: 'It's Only Me'
Mike Fox, Malcolm Hunt and Geoff Lawton
0 7134 8809 3
£17.99

For further details, please contact Sales and Marketing, Batsford, 10 Southcombe Street, London W14 0RA

www.anovabooks.com